I0406844

MY LIFE IS A
SURREALISTIC
NIGHTMARE

A COLLECTION OF ESSAYS, LYRICS, IMAGES & QUOTES BY

TONY
CARAVAN

MY LIFE IS A SURREALISTIC NIGHTMARE

by Tony Caravan

Copyright © 2016 by Tony Caravan

All original artwork, photos, typography and design by Tony Caravan
except where noted

Music performance rights through BMI (Anthony Caravan)

Cover artwork by Tony Caravan

All Rights Reserved.

ISBN-13: 978-1540766465

ISBN-10: 1540766462

First Edition

ROCKFLUX : Filmworks : Music : Publishing — Rockflux.com

THE (ORCHESTRATED) FALL OF MAN

There is a thin blurry line between science and science fiction. Anyone familiar with the works of writers such as Clarke, Asimov, Bradbury, Dick, Huxley or Orwell (among others) can attest to this. The intellects that produced works that accurately predicted space travel, communications satellites, robotics and social engineering were akin to modern day prophets. Beyond their fantasies, the details of how people and things would function in a time well beyond their time was truly visionary.

Similarly, physicists like Newton, Einstein, Curie and Hawking (and many, many more) predicted and detailed the mechanics of how things worked, in most cases, well before science could prove their theories.

In more recent times, CEOs of great technology companies like Jobs, Gates and Musk spearheaded the efforts to actualize the predictions and theories of the science fiction writers and physicists, respectively.

All of these individuals, and all of this work, was performed by people who were schooled in a manner much different than the education system currently in place in America.

Hold that thought, and let's flash back to a couple of thousand years or so ago, to a time where most people on this planet did not have an education. An era where kings, emperors and religious leaders controlled societies—centuries of bloody conquest, deadly diseases, despotic rule—leading to feudalism, colonialism and slavery.

Our ancestors did not have access to the knowledge of their time (or their past). Great libraries like the one in Alexandria[1] were restricted, and eventually destroyed. Only the elite had scrolls, and eventually books. The accumulated history of life on this planet was held by perhaps only several hundred—maybe a thousand individuals living in castles, estates or the Vatican[2]. The only

---

1 The Royal Library of Alexandria or Ancient Library of Alexandria in Alexandria, Egypt, was one of the largest and most significant libraries of the ancient world. It was dedicated to the Muses, the nine goddesses of the arts.

2 The Vatican Apostolic Library (Latin: Bibliotheca Apostolica Vaticana), more commonly called the Vatican Library or simply the Vat, is the library of the Holy See, located in Vatican City. Formally established in 1475, although it is much older, it is one of the oldest libraries in the world and contains one of the most significant collections of historical texts. It currently has 75,000 codices from throughout history, as well as 1.1 million printed books

exposure that the common man had to stories of the before times was limited to religious books or theatrical performances. The flow of information was controlled by the powers that be; and this lasted for a very long time.

Enter the modern era... Improvements in the printing process, the creation of the telegraph, then radio, and eventually television—all led to a broader dispersement of information to an ever-growing number of people. And with that knowledge, people started to question those ruling over them—both politically and religiously.

By the 1960s, people began to demand an end to social injustice and war. The civil rights, labor and feminist movements were in full force. People were starting to "turn on, tune in, drop out." The very fabric of society was unraveling—from the family structure to politics to the churches. People had once again eaten the, so called, forbidden fruit from the "Tree of Knowledge."

So just like so many years before, those self-appointed leaders of the billions of people on the Earth, decided they needed to intervene to squash the rebellion. And they did. There were political assignations, the Kent State killings, drug laws passed, mass arrests; and eventually an illusion of capitulation by ending the Vietnam War and enforcement of the Civil Rights Act[3].

But things weren't all exactly what they seemed... To replace the previous control over the masses by organized religion and the state; those that have always enslaved us had dreamed up a new form of domination. Their focus would now be on using the education system and information technology to maintain their power.

Soon they began to consolidate school systems—creating a hierarchy of administrators. Every school district now had administration buildings with, in many cases, more administrators than teachers. They controlled what books would be given to students, the curriculum, testing, structure of classrooms; basically, controlling every aspect of the education process—for both student and teacher.

Prior to this, a school consisted of a principal, a few office workers and a janitor. And as mentioned above, everyone from Albert Einstein to Issac Asimov and Steve Jobs to Bill Gates came up through this type of school system. In other words, the individuals

3 The Civil Rights Act of 1964 (Pub.L. 88–352, 78 Stat. 241, enacted July 2, 1964) is a landmark piece of civil rights and US labor law legislation in the United States that outlawed discrimination based on race, color, religion, sex, or national origin.

responsible for the modern world we live in, were schooled under an educational model that was declared obsolete and flawed. There's something wrong with that picture.

Over the following decades corporate-financial interests gained a stranglehold over the political systems in western civilizations. Countless laws were passed to benefit the aristocrats and enslave the populous. The media was used to sooth and divert the masses into believing that things were getting better. But with each passing year millions more people were struggling. There were endless wars, neglect of the infrastructure, increases in the "cost-of-living" and taxes. In effect, there was a return to Feudalism, though most were oblivious to it—due to government propaganda and media diversions. It has been called neo-Feudalism, wage-slavery, and a few other things; whatever you want to call it, it meant misery for the majority of people living on the Earth.

Then came the Internet... Suddenly, billions of people had access to information that previously was reserved for nobility—the stuff no longer taught in the public schools. All sorts of ideas about freedom and justice began circulating among the average Joe and Josie. They started to realize that maybe what they were taught in school, heard from politicians, and broadcast on the nightly news, wasn't the full story; and in many cases, wasn't even true. The potential for a 1960s-style revolution was brewing; and it had to be stopped.

So just as in previous times, be it despotic rule, organized religion, media propaganda or political double-speak; it was decided to use the very thing that had unleashed the seeds of rebellion to quell it.

Enter the smart-phone... While only in existence for a decade; it, along with Facebook, Twitter, Instagram (and all of the others), now consumed nearly every "free" if not waking, moment of the oppressed. The device, with its SIM card, tracked everyone, shared their private information with corporations and the government; but most importantly, kept them constantly busy and diverted by addicting them to living only in "the now." Whatever was trending, would spread like the old "wave" in football stadiums. Items would be posted and re-posted, tweeted and re-tweeted, liked but not capable of being un-liked. Finally those that have enchained mankind over the millennia had found the ultimate means of controlling the masses. Better than conquest and fear of torture, better than religion and the fear of eternal damnation, better than laws and threat of imprisonment—even better than mind control through media and propaganda. A simple rectangular device that fit in the hand or pocket of everyone would be humankind's undoing.

But the story doesn't end there... Blinded by technology, the maniacal megalomaniacs began to wallow in their achievement. They pursued more technologies to gain more information and control over their serfs. They even pursued eternal life through merging man with machine, artificial intelligence and nano-biological technology. But they missed one thing. In their relentless pursuit of more power and life-extension, they forgot that they were humans themselves. Through their own meddling with nature, they retarded the growth of the human brain, and the adaptation of their bodies to changes in the environment.

The overuse of drugs like antibiotics and anti-psychotics were creating super bugs and un-treatable brain disorders. The over-processing of foods were causing increases in heart disease and diabetes. There were shortages of fresh water, contamination of fish and farm animals. Cancer deaths increased. Technology was replacing jobs at a time when the population was growing almost exponentially. Poverty and hunger was on the rise. Endless wars created millions of refugees whose cities were turned to rubble.

And while all of this (and much more) was going on, people clung to their smart-phones and immersed themselves in their apps. Sometimes they would look up to binge watch on their HDTV, but they would quickly look down, so they could "share" what they were doing.

First came dystopia for billions of people—that is today—in the inner cities and rural America, on the African continent, in India, South America and throughout Asia. People dying of curable diseases or lack of food and water. People unable to work because there are no jobs. People being killed because of corporate-state interest in their land or resources. That is what is going on right now for billions of people on this planet. And it is spreading like a virus to more and more people, in more and more places, day by day.

There is no solution to this man-made disaster. There's no technology that is going to lift more than half of the world's seven and a half billion (7,500,000,000) people out of poverty and lives of desperation. And even if there were (and there are) solutions, they would/will never see the light of day, because the powers that be don't have a profit-incentive to make it worth their while to act.

There is no profit in health, only in treating diseases. There is no profit in allowing people to have access to fresh water, only profit in selling bottled water to them. There is no profit in allowing people to be farmers, when billions are being made by the agricultural conglomerates. Remember, corporations are in business to increase the value of their shares for their stock holders, not to save the world.

I put it to you now, that the extinction of humans has been brought about by only several thousand individuals. Those so self-centered, so intoxicated with power and the accumulation of material things, that they have lost all there is to be human. They are without empathy, and they are responsible for the suffering of billions of people on this planet.

And while there are those (like myself) that try to remove ourselves as much as we can from the dystopian society they have created for us; the oppressors continue to pick on us, over-charge us, tax us and regulate our every activity. Any freedom we have will be short-lived, because they are relentless in their pursuit of total control over every living thing and resource on this planet.

As I said many times before, I wish you a good existence, happiness where you can find it, and peace and harmony with nature. Seek the truth if you can find it. Eat healthy and try to stay stress free.

We had so much potential as a species, but I'm afraid that unfortunately we chose the wrong path. *Maybe next time...*

Tony Caravan
December, 2016

for the survivors

CONTENTS

ESSAYS

The (Orchestrated) Fall of Man .... FOREWORD
The De-Humanization of Man.. 17
Humans are Insane 21
Social Media is an Excuse to Avoid Being Social 25
The Future Came and Most People Missed It 29
Until We All Deal with Greed and Want
    Violence Will Get Worse 35
Media and Politicians are in Denial Over Hyper-Inflation 39
My Life is a Surrealistic Nightmare.. 43
The Only Thing You Have To Do is Eat 47
Living Cheap (and Green) 51
Social Security Checks Should Be Increased 55
Life and Death 59
Six Reasons Why You Might Be Brainwashed........................ 61
Live To Be 250... 67
The Problem with Advertising and Promotion....................... 71
The Trump Phenomenon.. 75

LYRICS

You Are A Wage Slave 83
Someday Soon.. 85
BIGGERDANDAT 87
I'm Tired 89
Hunter-Gatherer Life 91
The Big Questions.. 93
Despair 95
Self-Driving Cars... 97
Don't Panic.. 99
Game Over 101
Portrait 103
I Woke From The Dream 105
Planet X 107
In Another Time and Place 109
A Sharp Sword 111
Forgotten People.. 113
Holidays in Dystopia 115

TWEETS & QUOTES 117
About the Author.. 129
Other Titles.. 130

Copyright © 2016 by Tony Caravan

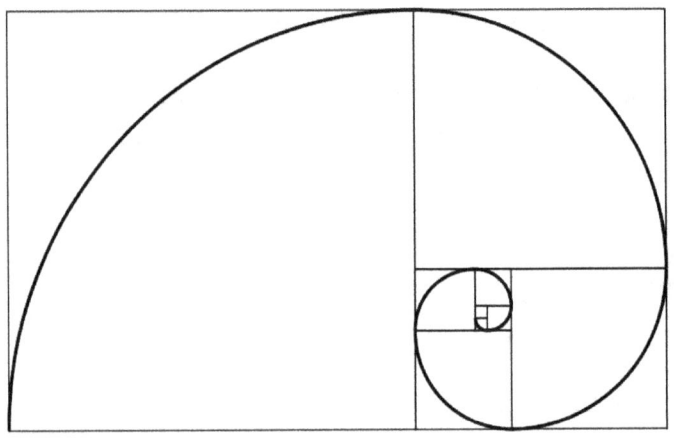

THE DE-HUMANIZATION OF MAN

Once homo sapiens started to have free time away from hiding from predators, or hunting and gathering; they began to ponder existence itself, and the world around them. Some used that time to figure out farming, irrigation and food storage, while others planned structures, communities and eventually created governments and armies to protect their territories.

At the same time there were those who used their extra brain capacity to contemplate the beauty of nature, the synchronicity and order of the universe, the perceptions of the senses, and basically, life itself.

Those individuals were the artists, architects, philosophers, astrologers, healers and teachers.

Initially, these "big thinkers" were held in high esteem by most people; but that didn't last very long.

Eventually, humans became greedy, envious, power-hungry and materialistic. They started fighting over everything from food and water sources to prime real estate and raw materials. This escalated into great wars. And as every advanced civilization and new technology came into being, millions were killed, and their cities turned to rubble.

This is our history right on through the 20th Century into the 21st. For every accomplishment that we have made, billions of people remain hungry, sick, without adequate shelter, or access to the advanced technologies of the day.

There is no empathy. There is no concern for the indigenous people who live on top of natural resources, or in areas of Geo-political importance to the power-elite that presently rule this planet.

And on top of that, most people aren't even aware of the amount of blood that was spilled for them to live where they do, wear the clothes they wear, have the devices they rely on, and live the lives they live.

We've de-humanized ourselves, and now we're moving to create artificial realities that don't even come close to the full sensory experiences of just living our lives.

Mankind's constant search for an alternative to flesh and blood existence either through the promise of metaphysical eternal life or through technology has been the biggest waste of time, resources and human lives in our tenure on this planet.

The fact is, there is beauty in truth and in nature and the cosmos. Artists have tried to depict and explain this throughout the millennia. But with each generation there is less and less interest in the arts. We're diverted by pop culture, the cult of personality—basically, we're in denial about practically everything.

The truth is, life itself is beautiful. You just have clear out the clutter, stop worrying about what other people have, do or want. Look at sunrises and sunsets and up at the stars in the night sky. Embrace another human being. hold them tight, and look them straight in the eyes. Taste the fruits of the land. Be human.

True happiness will never come about through wars of conquest or revenge; or through greed and materialism. We need to start living again as human beings, not cyborgs. Seek out "the truth (and it) will set you free."

Support the arts and the artists who strive to enlighten us.

True happiness will never come about through wars of conquest or revenge; or through greed and materialism. We need to start living again as human beings, not cyborgs. Seek out 'the truth (and it) will set you free.'

HUMANS ARE INSANE

Evidence points to a genetic design flaw in the human brain

Anyone with an iota of compassion can clearly see man's inhumanity toward man in every corner of this planet. And while some rationalize the madness of wars, social injustice, wage-slavery and wanton usury; there are no justifications for cruelty of any kind—not even for revenge, punishment or "pre-crime."

That is (should be) the stance of the sane person; but are any of us truly sane?

Everything in nature appears to have an obvious purpose for its existence—whether created or borne out of the natural order of things... The sun gives us light, heat and energy. An apple tree produces fruit that animals consume, and that also function as seed pods for the continuation of the species. Water sustains life within its volume, as well as through ingestion by living creatures. All things are interconnected in some symbiotic or synchronous way creating ecosystems and the micro and macro universe within us and all around us.

But what about humans? Where do we fit within this give and take world? We definitely take—there's no doubt about that. We kill for sport and material gain. We hoard material items that have no direct benefit to our existence. We hate and harm others simply because we disagree with their politics, ideology, or even their looks. We spend lifetimes living separate and apart from the flora and fauna co-inhabiting the Earth. *What are we even doing here?*

I reckon one can argue that we are a blight, or some kind of virus that exists to keep the planet from being overrun by other animals, plants, insects and bacteria. That would explain a lot about our tenure here, and the ruins of past civilizations of our kind. *Think about that for a moment...* Our history is full of civilizations that destroyed themselves or were destroyed by others. There are ruins scattered all over the place—in clear sight—but we treat them like historical monuments, instead of seeing the obvious fact that we are a self-destructive species incapable of living and working together in a continuous fashion.

Now all of that is scary enough; and it paints a pretty bleak outlook for the future of mankind and the planet. It's clear that conquest, slaughter, greed and self-centeredness is more the rule than the exception. But that's only part of the story. There are other things about us that demonstrate there's something wrong with our brains—they just don't work right. There seems to be something off about us, and the way we think.

First off, what happened before the "Big Bang?" Or, if you prefer, if God created all there is, what was there before God? If your answer is that God or the Universe always existed, then you answered the same as most people do. We have a brain that is capable of asking questions that we do not have the full answers to. And, unlike any other living creature (that we know of), we have thought processes that lead us beyond our capabilities.

We cannot comprehend how small a thing can be or the concept of infinity. We create mathematical formulas (like Pi[1]) that have no solution. Our modern physics is more like science fiction with things being in two places at once, there being multi-verses, multiple dimensions and distortions in space-time near Black Holes.

Many people believe there is existence outside of the physical body... a soul, spirit, energy force or continuum. We have the mental capacity to ponder these things, but we are unable to comprehend them. And, I'm not talking about "faith" here; I'm talking about the brain's ability to think logically about these things.

We are the only things, that we know of, that think of things, and act out on things, that either are existential to the rest of the stuff around us, or detrimental to ourselves and everything around us.

We are genetically flawed. We are freaks. We're halfway between having the potential to be beautiful caretakers that generate love, to forces of evil that destroy everything in their wake. Our brains are underdeveloped. It's almost like they're capped off from knowing the truth about ourselves, or our true purpose. And unlike all of the other "things" that surround us, we are disconnected and apart.

Yes, it is true, that there have been great philosophers and teachers that have imparted incredible wisdom in the areas of understanding, empathy, spiritual enlightenment, peace and harmony—and all of that stuff; but how few have listened, and how few have taken the knowledge to heart? And, even those whom have, still find the unknowable, unknowable.

---

1 The ratio of a circle's circumference to its diameter, equal to 3.14159265358979323846... (The digits go on forever without repeating)

Surrealistic Nightmare

There are nearly seven and half billion humans populating this planet right now; and that number is growing by the decade. In many of our lifetimes we will see nine or 10 billion people on the Earth. All of us vying for fresh water, food, a safe place to live, energy sources, material things and all of that.

The next great extinction is upon us—human extinction. Why? Because we're a flawed species. We're mutants, genetic freaks of nature—a blight on the living planet.

We are the only things, that we know of, that think of things, and act out on things, that either are existential to the rest of the stuff around us, or detrimental to ourselves and everything around us.

SOCIAL MEDIA IS AN EXCUSE TO AVOID BEING SOCIAL

A paean to human interaction

Obviously there are many aspects of digital communications that have enhanced our lives. And, as someone who has always embraced the latest technologies, I appreciate the tools that bring the world into the palms of our hands at the speed of bandwidth. That said, there is one aspect of the Internet that, to me, has been de-humanizing and counter-productive to our culture; namely, social media; and, in particular, Facebook®.

The way I rate any new invention, or process, is by first asking the question, is it necessary? Does it fill a void, and/or improve upon something that already exists? Next, does it do what it does without taking away from, or eliminating, the thing it was created to replace? In the case of Facebook®, and other social media platforms, the answers are yes and no.

While it is nice to share photos and comments with friends and strangers, neither of these are new or unique to the Internet. And, while it is also great to have your own "page" where you can chronicle your life story, that's nothing new either; blogs and personal websites have been around for over 20 years now. The same goes for messaging, sharing videos and forming Online "groups."

And if that's all Facebook® was, I wouldn't be writing this piece; but unfortunately, social media is far more than a means of sharing and communicating; it's become an obsession and replacement for human interaction. To be more specific, it has become an excuse to not call or visit friends and family members; and worse, a place where people can live in a fantasy world of reinvention and Photoshopped images to avoid looking at themselves in the mirror or being seen by others for who/what they really are.

I know there are all kinds of arguments racing around in your head right now, but I'm not talking about that stuff—yeah, I know what you're thinking... What I'm saying is that it has become so easy to not have real social interaction, that we're losing a vital part of what it means to be human.

Face-to-face encounters now only occur at the workplace or during the mating rituals at bars, restaurants and shopping centers.

Practically every other venture "outside" is usually dominated by the, all too familiar, face down at the smart-phone. We don't truly experience things like a beautiful day or a concert, we hold the camera up in front of the scene to share it; rather than taking in the full sensory immersive experience, which can only be had with both eyes and ears and focus on what's going on all around you.

It's the same with having the smart-phone with you when you do hang out with friends in the real world. The constant interactions to tweet, post, and share photos creates a distraction and distances us from the people we are with.

To me, there is nothing like being there—all in—and having the full memory of the experience in my mind, rather than a photo or video to remind me of a portion of the totality of the moments I missed out on, while looking down, texting or snapping a picture.

Does any of this matter? Not really... It's just an observation by someone trying to hold on to his humanity before it's all lost to A.I.

Social media is far more than a means of sharing and communicating; it's become an obsession and replacement for human interaction. To be more specific, it has become an excuse to not call or visit friends and family members; and worse, a place where people can live in a fantasy world of reinvention and Photoshopped images to avoid looking at themselves in the mirror or being seen by others for who/what they really are.

Surrealistic Nightmare

THE FUTURE CAME AND MOST PEOPLE MISSED IT

A Tale of Two Tomorrows

While most of us walk around with incredibly powerful hand-held computers a/k/a smart-phones; and, we wirelessly communicate and transmit data to others thousands of miles away, many people are still unaware that there have been similar technological advances that have occurred in other areas as well. One can even take this assertion one step further, and say that most people are still living in the 1980s or '90s despite all of the advancements that have taken place over the last several decades.

What I mean by that is, *take a look around you...* Unless you live in a multi-million dollar apartment complex in a major international city, chances are you are surrounded by old or abandoned buildings— even row homes, cracked sidewalks, pot-holed roads, rotting electric "telephone" polls, failing sewer lines, broken street lights, crumbling bridges, rusted and faded signs, older cars and equipment, trash everywhere, and poor and/or homeless people walking around in tattered, worn-out clothes.

Meanwhile, the talking heads on TV report on stories of wars around the world, refugee and immigration crises, shooting sprees, classified data leaks, privacy on the Internet, pandemics, and self-driving cars—to name a few. Most of which are not only tragic, but absurd occurrences in the second decade of the 21st Century.

You see, despite the latest smart-phones, HDTVs, A.I. headsets, and a host of accompanying apps and gadgets; most people ignore the fantastic breakthroughs in other areas affecting the human condition; mainly because they don't see them.

For example, the U.S. government (thanks to DARPA[1]) has (and has had) the capability to not only track, but to also see and listen to anyone at any location on the planet. This is not science fiction, or a "conspiracy theory," just a present day technological fact. There is also no longer any need for, so called, "conventional weapons." The military has laser, sonic, magnetic, robotic and space-based weapons

---

1 Defense Advanced Research Projects Agency (DARPA) is an agency of the U.S. Department of Defense responsible for the development of emerging technologies for use by the military. DARPA was created in February 1958 as the Advanced Research Projects Agency (ARPA) by President Dwight D. Eisenhower.

that can defeat any terrorist group, anywhere and everywhere—within a matter of weeks (yes, weeks). And, they can do it surgically, I might add, without destroying buildings, roads and bridges and killing or displacing innocent people. *Why is this not being done?* Because the weapon industry makes trillions of dollars, and is one of the few major manufacturing employers left in America. If there were no more wars or conflicts, they'd be out of business and the media and bloggers would lose their ad revenue (and story content), and most politicians wouldn't have anything to base their election campaigns on. So it goes unreported, or under-reported, and the average person has no idea that the technology exists to end all wars once and for all. —As a side note to this, the vast majority of UFO sightings are simply advanced aircraft funded by the taxpayers (not aliens from another planet or time-travelers).

The root of most social unrest and crime in America is due to economic inequality. And this goes way beyond race, religion, ethnicity and geographic location—it simply has to do with the high cost of living. The majority of people in this country are in debt. Some work two jobs and still can't pay their bills. It's been called wage-slavery, or modern day Feudalism (neo-Feudalism). Simply put, the cost to pay for the average rent or a mortgage, utility bills, TV service, high-speed Internet, cell phones, taxes, insurance, credit card interest rates, loans, personal items, food and medical expenses add up to more each month than the average person earns—forcing them to beg, borrow or steal to survive.

Most criminal acts are acts of desperation—fueled by despair or being backed into a corner. Something that the people in the corporate board rooms or the West Wing can't conceive of. Cops know this, but nobody ever asks them. In the minds of politicians, there are only people like themselves, people who have jobs, and all of the rest are bums or degenerates. They have no concept of what it's like to be working poor, or out of work and trying to support yourself and/or a family. But these same politicians give billions of dollars to their corporate (criminal) benefactors—money, by the way, which they pull out of thin air. Then, they proceed to raise taxes, fees and interest on those struggling to survive.

This is why there is so much violence—it's because of greed! The obvious question is, *is there a solution?* The answer is yes. Use the same digital technology they use to prop up the stock market and the U.S. Dollar—by literally creating money out of thin air.

Surrealistic Nightmare

The government should wipe clean all personal debt (or at least a portion of it). Imagine how the economy would grow in the years following that, and how many jobs would be created. And, the funny thing is, it wouldn't cost anything to do it; since money is fake (fiat currency[2]) or just a digital number on a ledger in "the cloud."

As for privacy, secrecy and government whistle-blowers and leaks... There are far too many secrets in a country that is supposed to have a "government of the people, by the people, for the people..." Common sense states that, chances are, if you are hiding something, or lying about something, it's not a good thing. On the flip side, the government already knows practically everything about you. You are tracked with your cell phone's SIM card, your Internet usage, your utility bills, car registration, driver's license, credit cards, etc... All records from your tax forms to what you purchase in stores and Online are accessible and cross-referenced by vast computer systems with algorithms that mine the data for the advertising industry, government think tanks, law enforcement and corporations. You cannot hide from "Big Brother" no matter what you do. There's really no such thing as being "off the grid" anymore.

The breakthroughs in medicine and nutrition are beyond your wildest dreams... Research in life-extension has yielded genetic treatments that can halt and even reverse the aging process. Those working in this field treat aging as a disease, not an inevitability of life. The prospect of people living well into their 120s and beyond is now a reality; and, we're not talking about being in a nursing home—the goal is to double or triple the average lifespan while maintaining a body that is still capable of doing all of the things you want to do. Will this technology be available to the average person? Don't count on it. The rich and famous are already being treated, and also don't count on the cures coming to a family doctor, pharmacy or grocery store, near you, anytime soon.

When I look at the crumbling infrastructure in this country it upsets me. Here are these architecturally well-designed buildings rotting away; while there are skyscrapers and "box" buildings going up everywhere. The reason for this is mainly because there are tax incentives and government grants for new construction, but nothing but hassles for people trying to renovating old buildings. If we were to spend a fraction of the money being allocated to build those new ugly, useless structures and spend it to fix the decaying

---

2 Fiat currency is inconvertible paper money made legal tender simply by a government decree.

neighborhoods and downtowns, what a wonderful use of taxpayer money, and what a tremendous way to create local jobs and support small businesses.

Lastly, when I hear and see people talking about self-driving cars it drives me nuts (pun intended). Obviously this is a ploy by the automobile industry to sell more vehicles and put the final nail in the coffin of mass transportation. This is the 21st Century for cryin' out loud! We should have modern, fast trains and even monorails that take people wherever they want to go. Want privacy? Bring back private coaches on the trains with TV and WiFi. The idea that a car equipped with a bunch of cameras and sensors is going to react better than (most) humans is ridiculous. Technology is great, but there are limitations when it comes to certain things. Before autonomous vehicles can become ubiquitous we'd need to upgrade the entire road system—including the side-streets and alleyways. I mean, take a look around the average city... Sensors or no sensors, there's nothing to sense on most of the roads out there. I don't know about you, but I regularly have passed mountain roads with missing guard rails, faded lane paint, missing signage, etc. This is another example of elitist promoting something that would only work in their "gated" communities or "cities on the hill;" but it's simply not practical in the rest of the country.

There are hundreds of other examples of how people—both rich and poor—have a warped view of the present day; and if we don't find ways to bridge the gaps very soon, we're all headed for a dystopian[3] future.

---

3 Dystopia is a word used for an imagined place or state in which everything is unpleasant or bad, typically a totalitarian, environmentally degraded, "post-apocalyptic" future.

Surrealistic Nightmare

The root of most social unrest
and crime in America
is due to economic inequality.

UNTIL WE ALL DEAL WITH GREED, AND WANT, VIOLENCE WILL GET WORSE

It's not (just) about dirty politicians, weapons, corporate greed, race and religion—though they all play a big part in the psycho-drama unfolding everywhere. It's about the people struggling to survive who are driven to do the unspeakable things they do.

Not everyone—but many people—are capable of horrific acts of violence when they are pushed into a place where they feel helpless and trapped. Examples would be a mother trying to protect her children, a family evicted from their home, someone who hasn't eaten in days, people threatened by others, or living in war zones—you get the picture... People respond differently to the struggles of life—especially when their lives take a turn for the worse.

In the U.S. over 40,000 people commit suicide each year—that's an alarming statistic! They find life so unbearable that they just give up completely. This is a real tragedy, and something you would never expect in such a prosperous nation.

Likewise, millions of people are arrested for petty theft... Stealing food at a grocery store because they are hungry, or to feed their children; robbing someone of cash or a wallet, and shoplifting items to pawn to pay a debt. These are acts of desperation by desperate people; and though that by no means justifies the crimes, it is a sad commentary on the structure of the societies in which they occur.

Under different circumstances, most of the aforementioned might not have occurred—especially if so many people weren't homeless, starving, victims of violence, under-paid and over-burdened with debt. Imagine that? Tens of thousands of people might still be alive, and millions need not have ended up in jail, or others need not have been assaulted or had their valuables taken.

But this problem goes way beyond the tragedies of suicide and larceny; what about murder?

In recent years, we have seen the rise of mass shootings, revenge killings, and terrorist attacks to an unprecedented level. Why is this? And why has it become accepted as just another story on the news or an excuse for politicians to raise contributions (and our taxes)? People mourn, argue about policies, tweet and post pictures and videos; and then a week or two later, it happens again somewhere else. The so called "people in charge" don't do anything of substance, and the media plays lip-service to the politicians double-speak.

Personally, I believe that all of these problems are rooted in greed and want. The greed of politicians and corporate contractors to make billions of dollars and live extravagantly; and the want of the average (working) person to be able to have a roof over their head, food to eat, and some stress-free time to spend with their family, neighbors and friends.

There is never a thought by the weapons manufacturers selling the bombs that destroy villages, that they will kill people's relatives and create a refugee crisis, or that maybe that the survivors might seek revenge. There is also never a thought by the affluent as they parade around on TV showing off their excess wealth to a population that can barely afford to pay their monthly bills.

We've reached a point in this inter-connected world of 24-hour news cycles and instant messaging where nothing goes unnoticed. Even the poorest of the poor in third world countries are aware of what's going on. They see the injustices and inequality on a satellite TV in a public place; or on a smart-phone (which are becoming ubiquitous). The gap between the rich and poor has not only grown, but it is blatantly obvious to most of the inhabitants of this planet.

Again, as I said in the beginning of this article, not everyone deals with these things the same way. However, it appears that more and more people are being pushed to their limits and reaching the breaking point where they snap out and harm innocent people.

No single politician can solve this problem; and certainly nothing will improve unless the media does their job and delves deeply into the causes of these rampant acts of deadly violence.

We all need to demand of the media and politicians that they explain why they are doing nothing to avert these tragedies. People have to stop supporting a war machine that with every bomb and bullet creates more hatred and fuels future attacks.

It's time to start talking about peaceful solutions to the problems around the world, and at home; and, it's also time to find ways to feed the hungry, house the homeless, get medical attention for the

Surrealistic Nightmare

sick and elderly, and to lower the "cost-of-living" to match the incomes of those who work, or who are on fixed incomes.

Unless we address the issues of greed and want, this world is going to spiral out of control until it becomes a surrealistic nightmare or dystopia. Actually for millions of people, like me, it already is.

There is never a thought by the weapons manufacturers selling the bombs that destroy villages, that they will kill people's relatives and create a refugee crisis, or that maybe that the survivors might seek revenge. There is also never a thought by the affluent as they parade around on TV showing off their excess wealth to a population that can barely afford to pay their monthly bills.

MEDIA & POLITICIANS ARE IN DENIAL OVER HYPER-INFLATION

The reason why you struggle so much

There used to be (and still is) this thing called "Cost-of-living adjustments" (or COLAs[1]), that was set up to counter the effects of inflation on workers (wages), people on fixed incomes like Social Security and Disability, consumer pricing, and to gauge the overall health of the economy. It was enacted in 1973 and supposedly is still the standard measurement used by the government to make its financial determinations. However, there was no COLA in 2016, and the increases have been pitiful over the past couple of decades.

COLAs are based on a flawed system called the "Consumer Price Index," or consumer prices for wage-earners and clerical workers. The flaw is that the real cost-of-living goes well beyond what it costs to buy a gallon of milk, or even a gallon of gas; in reality, it (should be) what it costs to actually live in the U.S.

As most people know, the cost of things in recent years has risen out of control. The cost of housing, medical care, insurance, telecommunications, automobiles, utilities, taxes, interest on credit cards and loans, student debt and even healthy foods, are so high that people have to get into more debt just to pay their bills. This is not just what is referred to as inflation, but what is sometimes called hyper-inflation.

But why do politicians and media pundits constantly tell us that the economy is in "recovery" and that there is little or no inflation? Well that's an easy one: it's the same reason they say that there is 4.9% unemployment when over a third of the capable people in the U.S. don't participate in the workforce—they're either lying or delusional—or both. Not to mention, that they also want to keep the lion's share of our taxes to pay their friends on Wall Street and to fund their endless wars that create more and more unrest around the world and here at home.

Fact is, there is a serious debt crisis in America and it is being totally ignored by the media. And it's also true that desperation caused by debt is contributing to violence everywhere. People who are not living on the edge and starving, don't go "postal" or become

---

1 A COLA is a Cost-of-living adjustment based on changes typically to the consumer price index (CPI). Salaries, pensions and benefits are typically adjusted annually to reflect the changes.

refugees, they tend to be happy, productive consumers—*yuk!*

So why would the government and media want to propagate a lie about the state of the economy, when they know that sooner or later that lie will be exposed? It doesn't make sense. I mean, surely they can see the violence all over this country and the refugees flooding into Europe, not to mention the turmoil it has created over there (and here for that matter). You would think the politicians would do what's best for the people that pay their salaries, and you would think the media would want to share the truth with the people that support their sponsors—you would think?

Well, I don't have an answer to that. It's a "a riddle wrapped in a mystery inside an enigma." What I can say is that it appears to be coming to a head. The average American is so much in debt that it is just a matter of six months to a year before they will start defaulting on their loans, credit cards and bills in record numbers—we're talking probably tens of millions of people here. When that starts to happen, the system will start to unravel, financial institutions will fall, and the media and politicians will all have an awful lot of egg on their faces.

As they say, it's not a question of whether or not it's going to happen, it's a question of when.

Is there a solution? Yes. And it's an easy one. All they have to do is bail out the people the way they bailed out the banks. I mean, they create money out of thin air anyway. A dollar is just a piece of paper that has a number printed on it; it's not backed by gold or silver or any hard assets. In fact, the U.S. dollar (and foreign currencies) are pretty much worthless, and backed more by debt than anything else.

How would this work? Simple: Each household would be relieved of up to $20,000 in debt. A one time "debt jubilee" if you will. This would be coordinated by the Federal Reserve and the U.S. Treasury Department. The result would be the ushering in of an era of prosperity that this country hasn't seen since after the end of World War II. And, the level of violence in this country would decrease a hundred fold.

If that were coupled with terminating the endless oversees wars, and using the military budget to promote global peace initiatives, we'd see a gradual cessation of violence and refugees, and eventually world peace.

Sound unrealistic? Not really. Anything is possible if people have the will and determination to take the necessary steps to make it happen. It's just a matter of greedy people getting over the fact that there will always be "deadbeats" that will abuse whatever system is in place. The choice is more about whether we (as a society) want to continue to live in a world of high crime, endless wars, poverty and disease; or if we're willing to "let go," and move toward a more harmonious and peaceful co-existence.

Each household would be relieved of up to $20,000 in debt. A one time "debt jubilee," if you will... The result would be the ushering in of an era of prosperity that this country hasn't seen since after the end of World War II. And the level of violence in this country would decrease a hundred fold.

MY LIFE IS A SURREALISTIC NIGHTMARE

It's 4 a.m. and I'm awake. Which can be expected for two reasons: first, I went to sleep at 8 p.m. to avoid watching the political debates; and second, because the coal trucks began speeding up my street—leaving soot in their wake—en route to the power plant that spews out toxins by the metric ton.

Yesterday I spoke with a representative of the local sewer "authority." They sent me a "10-Day Service Termination Notice." The woman on the phone coldly told me that unless I paid my bill, they would turn off my water. When I told her that I recently lost my job and could not pay the full amount at this time, she said that it was not her problem. When I also told her that this would create unsanitary and life-threatening conditions, she directed me to contact a charity. The bizarre thing about this is, I paid my water bill; and if they wouldn't have recently raised the sewer bill by nearly 50 percent, I probably wouldn't have gotten behind in the first place.

Later, I received a text on my cell phone threatening to interrupt my service. I've decided that I'm just going to let them turn it off. I've already looked into getting one of those VoIP jacks that you pay 40 or 50 bucks a year for phone service (and they have an app for WiFi calls, too). *So to hell with them...*

I tried to combine my TV and Internet service to save money, but they keep raising the prices and charging me for (their) taxes and for sports fees—*I don't even watch their gard-darg sports programs!*

Basically the cost of everything has risen beyond my ability to pay—and I live a very humble life, in a small house, in a crumbling neighborhood, in the poor part of town.

So there you have it, life in 21st Century America—the land of the slaves and home of oppressors. A place where those who've made billions off the backs of the hard-working taxpayers, keep raising the prices so they can have more. A place that wages war all over the planet so that global military corporations can make billions in profits to manufacture more weapons and more killing machines. A place where politicians are sock-puppets to Wall Street gamblers. A place where bankers print free money for themselves and charge ridiculous interest rates to the citizens. —*By the way, I canceled all my credit cards, too.*

Tony Caravan

What's even more insane are the talking heads on TV that support the power-hungry politicians and greedy financiers. Let's face it, the media is more to blame than the politicians. If they wouldn't parrot what comes out of Washington and the State Houses, maybe more people would see how this country has become one big tax farm—a return to the plantation days.

The violence and social unrest that we see on our city streets and around the world is preventable. Sure there are a plenty of criminals, gangs, some bad cops, racists—and all of that; but we also shouldn't be handing out guns so easily to psychopaths and sociopaths either. Moreover, as I've said over and over, if people weren't struggling to keep a roof over their head, and to feed themselves and their families, they wouldn't be constantly on the brink of snapping out. Stress not only kills the one under pressure, but it often boils over to those surrounding the tortured individual.

People have to shake off their cognitive dissonance and lives of diversion. Most of us are just a few rent increases and price hikes away from homelessness. Avoiding the reality that we are already living in a totalitarian dystopia is madness. *We are living in a totalitarian dystopia!* Just look beyond your furnished apartment or house or plush car interior and see the world that surrounds you.

And one more thing... Believing that a politician will save you would be laughable, if it wasn't so pathetic. Things have gotten progressively worse over the last several decades, and there have been both Republicans and Democrats "in charge."

The laws are written by the lobbyists who represent the corporations that own this country. Yes, I'm sorry to report that, we've been bought and sold years ago, and that all of that spectacle of the cyclical political media circus is nothing more than theater for your mind. You are being deceived, lied to and played for a fool.

Hey, the sun is starting to come out... Looks like it's going to be a nice shinny day! I hope my face doesn't melt.

People have to shake off their cognitive dissonance and lives of diversion. Most of us are just a few rent increases and price hikes away from homelessness.

TC's Famous Homemade Veggie Soup

ingredients:
Shiitake mushrooms, chopped broccoli, cauliflower, one sweet potato, carrots, sliced onions, 4 garlic cloves (diced), spinach, lentils, barley, ground flax seed, XV olive oil, apple cider vinegar (splash), ground pepper, turmeric, Sherpa salt, parsley, sage, rosemary, thyme, fresh oregano, basil, cayenne, hot sauce, soy sauce (dash), ginger, bouillon cubes (choice), linguine (cut for noodles), bay leaves (remove after)...

instructions:
Fill a large pot halfway with water and bring to a boil, then reduce to a simmer. Add all of the ingredients, cover and cook for about 30 to 45 minutes. Stir frequently. Let cool down a bit and eat. Refrigerate pot and re-heat for up to 3 days. Makes approximately 6 to 8 large bowls of soup.

THE ONLY THING YOU REALLY HAVE TO DO IS EAT

I had one of those "moment of clarity" thoughts the other day. You know, you see something, hear something, and then suddenly you are awakened to the absurdity in it, or your mind becomes aware of something that's been hiding in plain sight. In my case, it was the idea that the only thing we really have to do is eat (and drink of course). And yeah, I reckon you can argue that shelter is also important; so while you're at it, add in land, or a place to live.

Keeping that in mind, what kind of mad society have we created? Look at all of the ridiculousness we've generated around the basics of human existence... All of the complications, all of the things, all of the rules, laws, taxes, fees, fines and such-the-like.

Our lives have become surreal. We accept all of the absurdities thrust upon us as if that is the only way that things can be, and that it's the only way we can live. *So much for the "pursuit of happiness..."*

I've always believed that all people born on this planet are equal. Think about it... The moment of birth. There you were, naked and without any possessions. Your only thought was perhaps fear and a desire to be held by your mother, and then to feed. In those early days and weeks, we were all just Earthlings filled with wonder and the desire to learn, explore, be held and loved. A bank account, credit cards, material items, social standing, or cultural background doesn't mean anything to an infant. *That infant was you!*

Fast forward through the indoctrination of the school system and the rules and regulations of governments; and then being forced to labor in buildings, so you can have food and drink and shelter.

I don't accept that. And I believe it is our birthright to choose how we want to live our lives. If I want to grow my own food, and get my water from a well and rainfall; and, I'm happy to live on my land, in my house, without a car, or hundreds of material objects; I should be free to do so, and not forced to pay taxes and fees for the things I do not use, or even want.

As long as I do not infringe on another person's freedom, then I should be free to pursue the life I want. And that's not to say that those who want to commute to a 9-to-5 job in a building and be surrounded by gadgets and fancy furnishings, shouldn't be free to do what they want either. We both should be free to live as we like; again, as long as one or the other of us doesn't get in the way of the other person's right to do as they please.

I realize for many people this sounds crazy—especially in the 21st Century. And maybe I am a little crazy to think this way. But whether I am or not, I never agreed that society would have the right to dictate how I would live my life. *I signed no such agreement.*

I've come to the point where I'm happy not being a part of the rat-race. I don't have an overwhelming desire to own more things than I already have; and subsequently, have to give up more of my "free time" in order to pay for those things, and the interest on the credit cards needed to purchase those things. I also don't feel I should have to pay so much in taxes, when I don't agree with the corrupt politicians, or support their wars for oil and pipelines, or all the other things they do with most of the money they steal from us.

Which brings me back to the idea that the only thing you really have to do is eat. Everything else is just an elaborate construct by greedy and power-hungry humans so they can live (well) off the backs of the rest of us. All of us were born, and at one time, were next to each other in a maternity ward, naked and alone, without any of the trappings of this current society.

Do me a favor, tell your beloved politicians that I don't care about them, and that I quit. I'm not going to watch them on TV, and I'm not interested in their follies. Count me out. Leave me alone.

Oh, and by the way, I hope you enjoy the soup recipe...

The only thing you really have to do is eat. Everything else is just an elaborate construct by greedy and power-hungry humans so they can live (well) off the backs of the rest of us.

Surrealistic Nightmare

LIVING' CHEAP (AND GREEN)

Escape the Rat-Race
and Rediscover What it's Like To Be Human

I'm no gardener, but those veggies and herbs (at left) were grown in my humble backyard garden. The herbs were from seed packs that only cost a dollar; and the tomatoes were from seedlings that cost a couple of bucks. I've been eating lettuce, tomatoes, parsley, oregano, green peppers, jalapeño peppers, cabbage with corn on the way—everyday!

The thing is, it's easy and inexpensive to grow your own food, and you really don't need a lot of space—maybe about a 10' x 10' plot. And all you have to do, is to be willing to put in a little time weeding and watering. You'll find that the Internet is chock full of step-by-step advice columns and videos on how to set up a garden, plant, etc.

As for where to live, there are still plenty of places in this country (even close to cities and transportation) where you can buy a house with a yard in the $20,000 range or less. *Yes, I'm serious!* I bought a house for $16,000, and my mortgage, taxes and insurance (together) are only a little over $200 a month. Which is way less than the $650 a month I was paying to rent an apartment several years ago.

Do some searching on one of those Online real estate sites like Zillow or HomeFinder, and enter a price and an area you are interested in; and then view the listings from cheapest first. You'll be surprised what you find. It's true, you'll get a lot of results that are major fixer-uppers, in questionable neighborhoods, or remote areas; but if you sort through them all, and do a little research, you'll discover a few diamonds in the rough like I did. There are always people looking to unload houses cheap and fast because they are either moving or perhaps there was a death in the family.

The things I would look for (if it's not the greatest location) is whether the property is on a main road, well lit at night, next door to somewhat normal people, walking or hiking distance to a grocery store, doctor, etc. —Again, I found one that meets all of those criteria for next to nothing.

Having a yard—however small—is key. Besides having the space for a garden, you can set up a grill and a couple of lounge chairs and enjoy the great outdoors. *I got a great tan last summer!*

As for keeping the costs down, consider adding a wood-burning stove and a couple of solar panels to keep the utility bills low. Also, use a rain barrel to collect water for your garden—so you save on your water bill.

All you need to do is to earn enough money to pay your small mortgage, utilities, Internet and to buy necessary personal items —probably between $600 or $800. A part-time job, music, arts and crafts, or doing or selling something over the Internet should cover that. And with that low of an income, you qualify for free health care and food stamps. And hey, why not? The government bailed out the banks to the tune of billions—if not trillions—of dollars with taxpayer money; I say that qualifies us for a few of the table scraps. (I know some people will take offense to the food stamp thing, but think of it as a temporary bridge until your first harvest.)

The question you have to ask yourself is, do you want to be a wage-slave with debt-stress for your entire life; or would you rather live free and experience the joy of being human? I mean, who knows how much time we've got left on this planet? What, with all the insanity going on with wars, wanton acts of violence, insane politicians and corporate CEOs; not to mention the changes in the climate, the potential for pandemics, and a dumbed-down populous that seems to be constantly at each us other's throats…

Anyway, that's what I did—the "live free" thing, that is.

TC's Famous Salsa
mix together:
Garden-fresh chopped tomatoes (or a can of fire-roasted), sliced 1/2 of onion, 4 garlic cloves (diced), two thinly-sliced jalapeño peppers, one half roasted red pepper, Sherpa salt, cilantro, cumin, fresh oregano, basil, parsley, cayenne pepper, paprika, relish, Frank's® Red Hot Sauce, Tabasco®, turmeric, fresh ground pepper, ginger, flax seed oil (dash), XV olive oil (to fill out bowl). Serve fresh.

Surrealistic Nightmare

The question you have to ask yourself is, do you want to be a wage-slave with debt-stress for your entire life; or would you rather live free and experience the joy of being human?

SOCIAL SECURITY CHECKS SHOULD BE INCREASED

We've got it all backwards in this country...

The idea that those who worked hard (and paid into Social Security through payroll taxes) for 40, 45, or even 50 years, should not have enough retirement income to pay the basic costs-of-living is cruel and unusual punishment for the citizen taxpayers of this country.

What's wrong with "the system"

First of all, if interest rates were higher, the fund would increase exponentially through compounding interest[1]; likewise, people could have savings accounts that would also rise. The idea of market-based retirement accounts is absurd, since we all know that the market crashes several times over a person's lifetime—meaning they lose their retirement savings several times over.

Second, the Millennials are now starting to overtake the Baby-Boomers. Which means that (technically) there should be more people able to pay into the system than those who are taking out of it. The fact that U.S. businesses invest more into stock buy-backs than back into their companies, and that government wastes our tax dollars in foreign lands, and bailing out banks and insurance companies, is the true reason why there are fewer domestic jobs and subsequently less money going in to Social Security.

The excuse that people are living longer is not a valid argument either. It's the rise of healthcare and related costs that are putting the strain on the entire system. The cost of personal care facilities, rents, utilities, cable and Internet, phone and healthy foods has sky-rocketed in recent years. These abuses (government-approved) are the true reason why older Americans are suffering. The (promised) cost-of-living increases have not kept up with the real cost of living. Actually, they've been almost nonexistent. Basically, the government broke its contract with the American people, and squandered taxpayer money on folly.

We are the government!

We pay the taxes! Social Security is our retirement program! If the

---

1 Compound interest is interest added to the principal of a deposit or loan so that the added interest also earns interest from then on. Over time the original deposit increases many fold.

think tanks and bureaucrats want to come up with a new system for the next generation, go for it; but for the people who worked hard for their entire lives (and paid into Social Security), they deserve to get out what they were promised—an income that would sustain them when they retired.

Those who ignore that there are many millions of people who are already suffering because of the lack of increases in COLAs, are just downright evil. Most American workers don't have IRAs[2] or savings. They worked long-hours for their entire lives to build this country. To abandoned the majority of citizens is not only inhuman, but criminal.

People seem to forget that this is a representative government. Those in Washington are not "leaders," they are representatives of the people. Their job is to do our bidding. We are supposed to decide how our tax money is spent—not the politicians—they work for us! And as far as Wall Street, they don't deserve a dime of our money; in fact, it's time they started paying their fare share. They are private businesses. We've saved their collective asses so many times, it's time they either bail us out, or stop taking our tax money.

This issue is growing daily and will probably come to a head within a year—especially as millions more older Americans are forced out on to the streets, or to live in extreme poverty; all, after a life of hard work and service to this country.

It's unbelievable how we have allowed a ruling class of oligarchs to take over this country and push us back into an age of wage-slavery and suffering not seen since the Middle Ages.

---

2 Individual Retirement Accounts usually linked to stocks and bonds.

Millennials are now starting to overtake the Baby-Boomers.
Which means that (technically) there should be more people able to pay into the system than those who are taking out of it.

photo: T. Levitz

Surrealistic Nightmare

LIFE & DEATH
What are we doing with our lives?

A very dear cat acquaintance of mine passed away the other day; and, as anyone who has befriended an animal knows, the amount of joy an animal can bring into your life is unmeasurable—not to mention the companionship of another living being that looks into your eyes and enjoys just hanging out with you.

Naturally, I was overcome with grief, which exploded into weeping. Then I buried her in my back yard.

At the end of the day, as I reflected on the time I spent with her over the years, I realized how insane our lives have become.

We post about this, tweet about that, and constantly share photos of everything we do; and by consuming most of our lives with all of that, we miss out on living those moments. True, in one regard, we are preserving those moments; but by introducing a device and a procedure, we are removing ourselves from the full human-animal, living experience.

Unlike a photographer who objectively captures a scene, like an artist on a canvas; we are recording ourselves in that scene, and removing ourselves from the immersive experience—even if only for a short period of time.

In the end, we're left with thousands of photos and comments in the cloud that depict thousands of moments that were wasted by not being truly 100 percent there.

Only when we lose a friend, the subject matter of our obsessive social sharing, do we realize that all the photos in the world can't recreate the physical moments gone by.

For many this may not make any sense, but for me, I intend to spend more time living and less time with that rectangular piece of glass and metal in my hand.

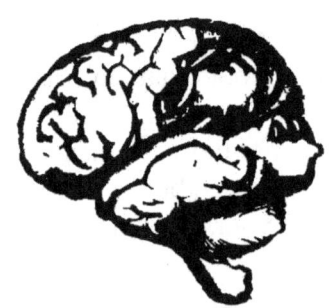

SIX REASONS WHY
YOU MIGHT BE BRAINWASHED
The things you think you know might be wrong.

This is not about conspiracy theories or fringe science, this is about how our minds have been molded and twisted from grade school right on through to most of what we are exposed to by the media as adults. For some people this information will be shocking; and they may respond with cognitive dissonance, for others it will be refreshing to read someone else articulating what they've felt inside all along.

1) You believe that the U.S. economy is in "recovery" and that the Stock Market is booming

Despite what you read and see on the nightly news about the Stock Market rising; the U.S. economy is in the worst shape it's been in since the Great Depression. Not only is the Stock Market a false barometer of the state of the economy, it's nothing more than a casino for the wealthy, and a means of money-laundering for banks and corporations. Most stock prices are falsely inflated by companies buying back their own stock instead of investing in their firms. The effect of this charade is that businesses are failing to spend money on updating equipment, research and development, hiring employees and complying with safety regulations. The result is companies that look good on paper, but that in reality they are decaying, losing money, market share, and falling behind their foreign competitors. It's just a matter of time before many of them implode and go bankrupt.

The Federal Reserve (an entity comprised of private banks which has nothing to do with the government) creates money out of thin air—*yes, literally!* Banks are given this money at little or no interest, and it is then used to buy bonds, which is just another word for debt. Subsequently the U.S. dollar is not backed by hard assets like gold or silver, rather it is a worthless piece of paper (based on debt) that has a perceived value only. Likewise, the inflated value of real estate is not based on the integrity of the structure, materials used, life expectancy of the building, or any of those things; it's merely a price set by speculators that has no stability whatsoever. It is inevitable that there will be another real estate bubble burst in the near future.

When you combine companies that don't contribute much to the economy as a whole (or pay much in taxes) and add that with trillions of dollars of debt based on loans that will never be paid, properties that are worth a fraction of their real value, insurance companies that are barely able to pay out their claims, and a government spending more than it brings in, year after year, you see the economy the way it truly is—in a shambles, and on the verge of collapse.

2) Unemployment is the lowest it's been in years...

Actually, real unemployment is the highest it's ever been. Over a third of the people who are capable of working are currently not working. That means that real unemployment isn't under five percent, rather it's over 30%. Not only that, but unemployment figures are based on the number of people applying for, or receiving unemployment compensation. Once a person has exceeded their time of receiving benefits, they are no longer counted as being unemployed—even though they may still not be working. In addition, many of the jobs that have been created over the past decade or so have been in the service industry, or temporary or part-time positions. The idea that there is close to full employment in the U.S. is so far from the truth that it's unimaginable how news anchors and politicians can repeat that lie, over and over, with a straight face.

3) We live in a democracy and elections and politicians matter

Technically the U.S. is a Democratic-Republic which basically means we have a representative government. In other words, we supposedly elect individuals to go to Washington and implement the policies that "We the People" want. To state it differently, the President is supposed to be our stooge in the White House, not some worshiped "leader." Unfortunately, due to corporate tampering with the system, and the creation of a "power-elite class," the people now have very little say in how their government is elected and run. It started with gerrymandering, where politicians warped the voting districts to favor their re-election. Next, the Supreme Court ruled that corporations had the rights of individuals, which opened the flood gates of campaign contributions—which a greedy media embraced—thereby handing over the control and flow of information to those with the most money (Remember, even the populist candidate Donald Trump was only able to afford to campaign because he was wealthy, and won the Republican Party's nomination.). The results are well-produced multi-media political propaganda campaigns that are deceptive and mess with people's minds. In the end, the people know very little about who the person they are voting for truly is, and what they will do when they get in office; and, they know even less about what that person is doing right now, in their name, with their tax-dollars.

4) The U.S. is a "force for good" in the world...

Would that this were true... For decades the C.I.A., and other governmental entities, have been involved in political assassinations, foreign government coups, occupations, colonialism and supporting terrorists groups. This is hard to believe for most people, but all you have to do is spend a little time researching the history of South and Central America, Africa, the Middle East and Southeast Asia, and you'll uncover a wellspring of unclassified, historical facts that go against everything you were ever taught in school, heard on the news, or that are still bandied about by people everywhere.

When you hear a politician say that they are taking some military action to "protect our interests," what they really mean is that they are doing the bidding for some corporation that has an interest there. Most know about wars for oil and pipelines, but we've also killed thousands upon thousands for land, crops, water, drugs and the almighty dollar. For example, few know that Afghanistan was more about an oil pipeline and keeping the poppy fields than it was about the Taliban. The same goes for Syria—Qatar and Saudi Arabia want a gas pipeline through there. Iraq wasn't just about oil, it was more about Saddam Hussein wanting to sell oil in Euros instead of U.S. Dollars. And nobody even talks much about the massacre going on in Yemen, with Saudi bombers being re-fueled by the U.S., who also provides targeting intelligence.

The U.S. has become an imperial power, or an empire, if you will. The idea that former President Obama was awarded the Nobel Peace Prize is disrespectful to every other recipient throughout history. Under the Obama administration there were more drone bombings of civilians at wedding parties, hospitals and public spaces—with thousands of innocent casualties. Our government has supported dictators and repressive regimes across the globe. Practically every news report on violence abroad is missing one key component, that somewhere at the heart of the heinous acts and atrocities committed is the hand of you know who. *Why can't we be a force for peace? Have we given up completely on diplomacy?*

5) The Department of "Defense"

One of the biggest lies perpetrated upon the American people is the concept of the Department of Defense. As if they have defended us, or their purpose is, to defend us. More than half of our tax dollars go to the so called defense budget, yet over the past several decades they have failed to defend us on numerous occasions. Remember the USS Cole, or how about 911—they sure didn't protect us from that. What are they doing with the trillions of dollars we give them? In recent years there have been terrorist acts right here in the U.S., not to mention horrible shootings and bombings in Europe against our allies. They should be honest and change the name to the Department of War. Actually it used to be called that years ago. At least then they were being truthful about their intentions.

I realize this is a touchy issue with some people, but it shouldn't be. This isn't saying anything negative about the men and women in uniform. This is calling out the Pentagon and the military contractors that have made America, and the world, less safe for the sake of making trillions of dollars in profit for military contractors. They don't want peace, because peace means they're out of business. *Man, is that sickening.* How do they sleep knowing that the money they make comes from charred bodies of babies and bombed out houses, refugees and dismembered soldiers and innocent people caught in the crossfire.

We have so many submarines, nuclear missiles, battleships, destroyers, cruisers, bombers, satellites, high-tech weapons and more, that we can cut our military budget in half and still maintain total superiority over the planet with money to spare to provide services to our veterans. If we just stopped the waste and messing in places we shouldn't be messing, we'd have hundreds of billions of dollars left over to spend on the American people and our own crumbling infrastructure and health care system. As far as I'm concerned, that's "defense" too.

6) The future will be bright and things will be better for everyone...

They've been spoon-feeding us this one forever... The fact is, with each passing year, less and less people have access to the breakthroughs in science, medicine and technology. Tens of millions are still without health care in the U.S., and many of those with, have high co-pays and deductibles. There are cures and treatments for all kinds of diseases, but most are out of the reach of the average person. The same goes for healthy foods and herbs—most are too expensive for the average working class family.

You see news stories about all of these things that will exist in the future... *Do you really think that you'll be able to afford them?* Already the cost of high-speed Internet, the latest model HDTVs, computers—even cell phone service, are all starting to become out reach to most people—except by getting into more debt to purchase them. The price of cars and trucks have doubled over the last couple of decades, but wages haven't doubled. The cost-of-living—especially rent—is now so high that working has become more like slavery just to survive and keep a roof over your head.

We've reached a point where there are so many people that the corporations only need a third or half of them to maintain their profits and stockholder lifestyles. For those who are no longer needed, there is no concern. The government, bankers and corporations have taken everything we have (to get where they are) and now they are starting to discard us. Just listen to the reporters and politicians talk... Do you think they are talking to you?

At this juncture, the best thing you can do is to hold on to your humanity, and not get caught up in the lies and propaganda being spewed out of the media. While I don't believe that it's possible to change the out of control system that's taken over, I do believe it is possible to change ourselves and to live better lives.

Despite what you read and see on the nightly news about the Stock Market rising; the U.S. economy is in the worst shape it's been in since the Great Depression.

Surrealistic Nightmare

LIVE TO BE 250
Longevity is not as rare as you may think

There was a man in China who reportedly lived to be 256 years old. Some records have him being born in 1677—the year Milton wrote Paradise Lost. He was 12 years old when Peter the Great became Czar of Russia, and over 100 when the Declaration of Independence was written. He was 200 after the American Civil War, and would live on to see electricity, cars, planes, and even World War.

He lived an active life until his death in 1933, working as an herbalist. He lived off a diet of lingzhi, goji berry, wild ginseng, he shou wu and gotu kola, and he drank rice wine.

There's a Nigerian man who is believed to be 170 years old, and an Ethiopian farmer claiming to be 160. A man in Indonesia has official identification showing his birth date to be 1870.

The world's oldest woman (on record) lived to be 122, and remained mentally intact until the very end. She smoked two cigarettes a day, had a diet rich in olive oil (and also used in on her skin), drank port wine, and ate over two pounds of chocolate per week. She attributed her longevity to remaining "calm."

There are many others from all parts of the world, all nationalities, and living in all climates and elevations. Many of the oldest people do not necessarily eat the healthiest diets or exercise beyond their normal daily activities. Many also drink alcohol.

Ancient writings speak of people living to be 800 or more—though these are dismissed as mere myths.

There are those in the scientific community frantically working to create nano machines to repair cells and reverse the aging process. Still others are desperately trying to figure out a way to transfer their human consciousness into a computer, so their minds can live on indefinitely (in a machine).

Like so many pursuits of modern man, these technological solutions to biology are foolhardy.

It is accepted by most in the medical profession, as well as by academics studying such things, that the three major contributors to death are stress, poor diet and lack of physical activity. Three things that our contemporary society forces upon us.

From an early age we are forced to sit in classrooms for the better part of the day, and fed foods high in sugar and fats. As children we are taught that life is a struggle and that we must achieve, succeed, and win. From scholastic competitions to climbing the corporate ladder, there's no end to that struggle. We are taxed and charged fees and interest that create more stress—dealing with debt and more debt on top of debt.

Ultimately, most people die of heart disease or strokes caused by stress, poor diets and a sedentary lifestyle.

This is no great revelation. It should come as no shock to anyone. The fact is, our societal structure is killing us; and if there ever are any technological breakthroughs in longevity, they will never trickle down to the average person, the same way that the bank bailouts never trickled down to the wage-slaves and taxpayers who footed the bill.

My advice to those seeking a long, fruitful and happy life is to get out of the rat race as soon as possible. Find a place where you can live relatively inexpensively. Get rid of all the extra clutter—those things you store or carry around with you everywhere. Eat healthy, take more walks, and avoid stress at all costs.

It's all about experiencing life as a human being. Feeling the sun on your face, looking up at the stars at night, having face-to-face (in-the-flesh) conversations with other people; and just having fun.

You don't need vitamins, a credit card or an SUV to live a long and happy life; you just need to rediscover your humanity.

From an early age
we are forced to sit in classrooms
for the better part of the day,
and fed foods high in sugar and fats.
As children we are taught that
life is a struggle and that we must
achieve, succeed, and win.
From scholastic competitions
to climbing the corporate ladder,
there's no end to that struggle.
We are taxed and charged fees
and interest that create more stress—
dealing with debt and more debt
on top of debt.

Reader note:

Some of you may wonder what this article is doing here... Well, once upon a time, I was a Creative Director at an ad agency. And I can't tell you how many times people ask me for advertising advice. *So here it is...*

THE PROBLEM WITH ADVERTISING & PROMOTION IN THE 21ST CENTURY

Ask most people who are trying to promote their small business or an event and they'll tell you that it's both expensive and/or very time-consuming. Unless you already have a captive audience who are tuned in to your every tweet and/or post (and that doesn't apply to most—especially in smaller markets), you have to resort to spending a ton of money on a combination of over-priced traditional media—radio, TV, billboards, magazine and newspapers—along with Google and social media ads. And even with all of that, the likelihood of reaching your target audience is still a crap shoot.

Gone are the days when you could advertise or partner with a radio station that "everybody" listened to. Now you've got people listening to everything from their private MP3s on iTunes, Google Play and Amazon Prime to Pandora, Spotify and the dozens of other stations and music sources. And while broadcast radio is still listened to in major markets during "drive time[1]" to and fro work, it requires an expensive "flight[2]"—a minimum of multiple spots per day over two weeks or more to reach the optimum amount of listeners.

Television still kind of works for national advertisers and smaller market cable buys; but with so many people choosing to watch on-demand or binge-view at a later date, timely ads don't work; plus, a lot of potential prime customers (who have disposable incomes) pay extra to opt out of commercials altogether with services like Hulu or Netflix. So don't count on TV unless you have money to burn.

Newspapers and magazines have lost a considerable amount of readers over the last decade or so; though they have managed to hold on to people who want to be informed. The demographic for daily newspapers is skewed pretty much over 40; while weeklies and magazines tend to each have their own niche group. If you are fortunate enough to have a product, service or event that matches the demographics and/or audience of a print publication, then compared to television or radio, it's probably the most cost-effective. But that said, because of the decline in readership over the years, you'll still be missing a bunch of people.

---

1 Drive Time is the time people spend in their cars going to and from work.
2 Flight is term used by media sales people to designate the duration of the ad run or campaign.

Then there's social media—a misnomer if ever there was one. Facebook®, Twitter® and the legions of other platforms to post comments, share thoughts, reactions, photos and such-the-like are mainly self-centered and voyeuristic. And while people tend to be followers of trend-setters, they don't react well to businesses or individuals trying to advertise or promote something to them on their private Facebook or Twitter page. Not only that, but even when an item of interest makes it to a person's "feed," it is quick to get buried in an endless scroll of tweets, re-tweets, posts, comments, pics and gifs from their countless friends and followers. Trying to use social media as the sole means of marketing your business or event is as about as effective as wearing a t-shirt with the same information on a crowded street—some random people close to you will notice; but who knows if they are even interested, or if the message even applies to them. YOU MIGHT WANT TO RE-READ THIS PARAGRAPH.

In the end, what it boils down to is that you're screwed if you have a limited ad budget and want to reach a broad audience. And despite all the hype about social media (or should I say the virtual reality playground) it's pretty much a waste of time—especially if you buy ads on it. Again, I'm not talking about big national advertisers here.

In an effort to create a homogenized culture, with a handful of media companies and mega-corporations in control of mass marketing and information dissemination; the "powers that be" have pretty much changed the landscape of advertising and effectively closed down most local media outlets.

Unless you have a big budget, you need to resort to labor-intensive "guerrilla[3]" marketing tactics to get the word out these days.

That said, having been a publisher of entertainment magazines, a radio station general manager and ad agency creative director, my humble advice is as follows:

Plan A) If you have a reasonable advertising budget. Purchase a select amount of cable channel ads (pick only stations that match your potential customer's demographics) over a two-week period. If there's a radio station that is popular with people who buy your products or services, then see if they have a "package deal" that gives you some primetime spots along with random (or "run of station" commercials). Also advertise in a niche publication (if there is one

---

3 Guerrilla marketing refers to people on the streets passing out things and orchestrating publicity stunts

in your area). Get your regulars and "friends" to post fun photos of your business or event to social media; but don't try to over-sell to people—it has to appear un-staged and natural. A combination of these efforts within a month of your event, along with passing out flyers and putting up some posters (nicely graphically designed), will get the best results. If you can find a cheap billboard, go for it.

Plan B) If you don't have much of an ad budget at all, then drop the cable and radio ads and just find a monthly or weekly entertainment publication and put a small ad in it. Get everyone you know to get involved passing out flyers and putting up posters wherever they can. Try to get free publicity through press releases or aligning yourself with a cause or a business organization. Get actively social with video clips, cool photos of people having fun (again, nothing staged), and try to get honest testimonials and comments by people that other people view as trend-setters or just regular Janes and Joes. Make sure you get a graphic designer involved to help create a "brand" that is memorable and communicates your message. And don't forget to keep the flow of photos and posts going during the event and after. This will insure that those that didn't make it the first time, will want to be there the next time.

Additional notes: I didn't include Direct Mail (which I do find to be effective), mainly because it can be quite costly. However, if you have the budget, I would encourage mailing out nicely designed graphic pieces. As for "spamming," I have a personal aversion to the whole idea; but in certain instances (where people actually sign up or "opt-in"), it might be worth adding to your marketing mix—depending on your target audience size and the market. *I hope that helps…*

"Unless you have a big budget, you need to resort to labor-intensive "guerrilla" marketing tactics to get the word out these days."

THE TRUMP PHENOMENON

**Understanding why Trump was elected,
the difference between an "alpha male" and a misogynist,
and the fear of foreigners versus racism**

In the post 9/11 era—which for tens of millions of Americans was most of their childhood and/or young adult lives—we were bombarded by the media and politicians with a fear of non-white people of non-European descent; in particular, those from the Middle East. After all, we were told that they somehow snuck into our country to perpetrate those unspeakable acts of terrorism we all watched played over and over on our television sets.

If that wasn't enough, in the build up to the wars in Afghanistan, Iraq, then Libya and now Syria, the daily drumbeat by pundits and government press agents has been that the "evil doers" are everywhere and they must be stopped.

The TV is chock full of images of refugees flooding into Europe and bombs going off in cities. There are countless stories of women being raped and assaulted by "these people." This stuff is all over newscasts, social media and flowing out of the mouths of government officials and the, so-called, mainstream journalists.

They also constantly warn us that these same foreigners want to do us harm here; and that we must be vigilant. They have also shown us over the years, how our borders are porous, and if drug dealers and human traffickers can get through, then so can the terrorists. This is the message we have been given.

Now taking all of that as a backdrop, is there any wonder that those who were scarred to death by 9/11, and those who were trained to fight that enemy overseas, along with the families of those patriotic men and women, as well as the people at home watching and hearing all of this constantly; is it any wonder, that they would be afraid of foreigners, and even harbor feelings of hatred for what they did, have done since, and what we are told they will do again?

This is the root cause of the xenophobia[1] spreading throughout the U.S. and Europe. It's symptomatic of years of conditioning us to support the war efforts and protect the homeland. What you have to understand here is that the majority of Americans are downright

1 Xenophobia is an intense or irrational dislike or fear of people from other countries.

scared. Scared of the unknown, scared of people of different cultures, people of different religions, fear of people of different skin colors. They're afraid of losing their jobs, their way of life—even the lives of themselves and their families. Yes, people are downright frightened of what this world is becoming.

Not ALL of these people are racists and xenophobes; in fact, the majority of Americans live, work and socialize with people of other races and creeds all the time. Inter-racial, inter-religious, and inter-cultural marriages are at an all time high in the U.S.

So what is all this talk in the media, and at protest rallies, about Trump supporters ALL being racists?

Trump received approximately 60 million votes; and, as we all know, there were surely tens of millions of Trump supporters that simply didn't vote—just as there were tens of millions of Clinton supporters who never went to the polls. The point is, perhaps as many as 80 million or more people found common ground with the message Trump delivered. And the fact is, there are not physically that many uneducated, poor, prejudice, white men of voting age in this country.

The vast majority of Trump voters were mostly people who wanted change, or didn't trust Hillary Clinton, or they were afraid that their cities might start looking like those European cities they see on the news. In short, they are a product of the news media and (establishment) government that planted these ideas into their brains over the last decade and a half. And, the fact that under an African-American president there seemed to be more violence against Blacks and imprisonment of people of color than ever before, Trump surprisingly had notable support from these constituencies—though this remained under-reported, and is shocking to many people.

As for the man himself... His actions, his associations over the years, as well as his pontifications from the pulpit don't paint him as racist; rather as a man with the same fears of tens of millions of other Americans. Did he/does he have supporters who were/are racists? Most definitely. Could he have been more outspoken against them? Yes. However, in the end, as he mentioned in his acceptance speech, he pledged to work for ALL Americans; and I'm afraid, that in this area, we're going to have to give him the benefit of the doubt, whether we like it or not.

On a slightly positive note, he did visit the Mexican president during his campaign; and the Mexican president also called him and congratulated him on winning the election. Trump has also made several pro LGBT speeches—though I don't recall those ever being shown or quoted in the media. All we can hope is that Trump-the-negotiator triumphs over Trump-the-campaigner. Either way, I believe, that when push comes to shove, the solution to immigration and diversity in America will be solved pragmatically, not radically—no matter who is in the White House.

Next to the women...

A misogynist is defined as a person who dislikes, despises, or is strongly prejudiced against women, in another words, a woman-hater. Trump, may be many things, but one thing he is not, is a woman-hater. In fact, Trump loves women, he's infatuated with them—both physically as well as intellectually.

He surrounds himself with women, his companies have women in power positions, and he loves his wife, sister, daughters. Even his campaign manager was a woman.

What Trump is, is what is referred to as an "Alpha Male." Some people might know these types as jocks, extroverts, high-achievers, over-performers; and yes, political leaders. This type of individual is usually a "player;" meaning, someone who dates a lot of women, has had many sexual encounters. Jack Kennedy, Bill Clinton—even Martin Luther King, Jr.—all had their share of questionable encounters with many females. The type of woman attracted to these men is usually one who is drawn to success, money and power.

What I'm trying to get at here is that, Donald Trump is a gregarious, braggart with a trash mouth. His "locker room" remarks are the kind of thing that most guys growing up heard from guys like that in high school, college through to the country club. It's distasteful, crude and wrong; but it's mostly just talk. It's just the kind of talk that most women find abhorrent (and rightly so).

Now please, don't take this as some sort of paean to Trump. It's just with so much focus on the words "racist" and "misogynist" in the media, I felt the need to clarify the terms as they apply to the guy. Too many times the media focuses solely on the flaws that can be sensationalized for headlines, instead of researching, analyzing and reporting on policy proposals and how they will affect us all.

Apart from the (many) negatives about Donald Trump, the strengths of the man are in his negotiating skills. He has pledged to work with other nations to find solutions other than endless wars; which, in and upon itself, was somewhat refreshing to hear. And whether he succeeds or not, he's also at least talking about trying to fix the crumbling infrastructure in this country, deal with the Wall Street robber-barons, improve the health care system, get veterans the aid they need, along with a litany of other things in his platform.

I know some are saying, "this guy's going too easy on Trump," but I'm really not. I'm just fed up with the media obsessing over the wrong issues. I'm suffering like most other people in this country. I can't afford to pay my bills. I'm a few missed payments away from losing my house or having the water and electricity turned off.

I want representation in Washington that will challenge Wall Street, that doesn't want conflicts with every nation around the world. The kinds of things that bureaucrats are suppose to do.

Personally, I don't think that any politician is the answer; and I also think there's a limit to the damage they can do. The most powerful force in this country is still the media; and until the mainstream media moves the discussion to the struggle of life for most Americans, we're screwed no matter who sits in the Oval Office.

We already have laws on the books regarding civil rights. And we've seen that, even under an African-American President, racial violence and inequality increased throughout the country. The reason for this is that the real problem is with the people, not the lawmakers. It's more of a societal issue than a political one.

I strongly believe that if we could eliminate the stress of debt and struggle of life for most Americans, that eventually prejudice and inequality would fade away. Sure, it may take decades; but as long as people are suffering, they will find someone to blame (or scapegoat)—which has always been the primary cause of this problem throughout history.

As corny as it may sound, the building of a better world has to start with you and me.

And, no, I didn't vote for Trump—I didn't vote at all.

As long as people are suffering,
they will find someone to blame
(or scapegoat)—which has always
been the primary cause of this
problem throughout history.

LYRICS

YOU ARE A WAGE SLAVE

by Tony Caravan

You are a wage-slave, you are a serf
You work your whole life, just to pay the bills
And when it's all over, you've got nothing but debts
You're destitute and broke, stressed out, sick and alone

The system is gamed, for those at the top
Elections don't matter; the politicians are mere puppets
They follow the commands, of their Wall Street masters

The democracy has fallen to Medieval oligarchs
Our society is stagnating through diversion and lies
The people are in denial due to media deception
Everything is backwards and nobody seems to care

We've sold our humanity for worthless paper money
for toys and trinkets and tasty treats
Life's become a game and we're just game pieces
The players decide who wins and who loses

For some who see through this dystopian world
The people at the top are buffoons and clowns
Life has become surreal—a sad, pathetic joke

But I'm not laughing
because there's too much suffering everywhere
Too many people are stressed and starving and disposed of
While the inhuman savages treat them like commodities

You are a wage-slave, you are a serf
You work your whole life just to pay the bills
And when it's all over, you've got nothing but debts
You're destitute and broke, stressed out, sick and alone

words and music copyright 2016 Anthony Caravan (BMI)
available on iTunes, YouTube, Spotify and most other online music sources

Tony Caravan

words and music copyright 2016 Anthony Caravan (BMI)
available on iTunes, YouTube, Spotify and most other online music sources

Surrealistic Nightmare

SOMEDAY SOON
by Tony Caravan

Someday soon now
we're gonna find out the truth
And very soon now
they'll be an end to the ruse

Then what's real will cancel out
all that we've been told
and the truth will flow
like a mountain waterfall
making its way for all to see

Someday soon now
the lies of those who repress
will be brought to light
And very soon now
the tyrannical manipulators
will be seen without their clothes

Then the world as we perceived it
will change right before our eyes
And the things we believed in
will fade away and die
giving way for a brighter day

Someday soon now
you'll understand what your
ancestors knew
You'll feel the life-force of
Mother Earth
and the energy of the Universe

Then as a Cosmic being
you'll comprehend the meaning
of pure love
And vibrate at the frequency
of peace and harmony with all there is

Surrealistic Nightmare

BIGGERDANDAT

by Tony Caravan

How we suppose to pay for this and that
when they over-charge us for everything else?
How do they expect us to act
when they're kickin' us down to the ground?

How we suppose to live
when we can't even afford the rent?
Who we suppose to believe then
when we know they're all tellin' us lies?

What we suppose to do,
when we got no jobs or place to go?

Where are they takin' this country?
What are they doin' to our land?

(chorus)
Biggerdandatnbetterdandat
Nuffadabullnlyincrap

All the politicians are shovelin' it
All the media are shovelin' it
All the corporations are shovelin' it
All the bankers are stealin' it
The goverment—they're stealin' it

Why should we fight their wars
when they're only 'bout sellin' weapons?
Why should we pay their taxes
when they only go to their wars?
Why should we believe anything they say
when smilin' faces tell lies?

(repeat chorus)

words and music copyright 2016 Anthony Caravan (BMI)
available on iTunes, YouTube, Spotify and most other online music sources

I'M TIRED

by Tony Caravan

I'm tired of politicians,
reporters and the so called news
I'm tired of superheroes
on TV shows and in the movies
I'm tired of wars and guns
and the military—rah, rah, rah
I'm tired of Facebook
and the showoffs on social media
I'm tired of cell phones
and selfies and texting
I'm tired of pop icons—splashed all over the place
I'm tired of the same music
year are after year
I'm tire of crime shows,
sitcoms and medical dramas
I'm tired of being overcharged
for everything
I'm tired of stuff not working
the way it should
I'm tired of paying taxes
and not having representation
I'm tired of games and apps
and over-hyped sports
I'm tired of thugs
getting away with murder
I'm tired of the lies
and the people who believe them
I'm tired of struggling
just to survive

continued

I'm tired of polluted air
water and traffic noise
I'm tired of being broke
and hungry and forgotten
I'm tired of promises
that are never fulfilled
I'm tired of watching
everything crumble around me
I'm tired of being bored
and annoyed
And now I'm tired
of this, too.

words and music copyright 2016 Anthony Caravan (BMI)
available on iTunes, YouTube, Spotify and most other online music sources

HUNTER-GATHERER LIFE

by Tony Caravan

(blues)
It's one thing to be a wage-slave
it's another to be broke
When you bring in less than things cost
you have to jump through hoops
just to survive

They constantly raise the rent
Up the insurance payment
Charge you interest and late fees
And threaten to turn things off

All you want is to stay in your house
To have running water
and a flushing toilet
Keep the heat on
And have a little food to eat

It's a non-stop struggle to survive
this 21st Century Hunter-Gatherer life
When you find yourself constantly behind
though you work harder and harder

You juggle the bills
Try to keep the utilities
from being turned off
Forget about luxuries
you'd be happy with the basics

It's never enough
no matter what you do and pay
They're always raising the prices
just enough so you can't afford to pay

continued

It's a non-stop struggle to survive
this 21st Century Hunter-Gatherer life
When you find yourself constantly behind
though you work harder and harder

It's a non-stop struggle to survive
this 21st Century Hunter-Gatherer life
Bargain hunting for this
gathering coupons for that...

words and music copyright 2016 Anthony Caravan (BMI)
available on iTunes, YouTube, Spotify and most other online music sources

THE BIG QUESTIONS

by Tony Caravan

I'm asking The BIG Questions like:
How did all of this begin?
How long can humans really live?
Are there cures for those really awful diseases?
Why can't we figure out infinity?
What is Dark Energy and Dark Matter?
What was Tesla trying to tap into?
Why did the ancients obsess over
the Procession of the Equinoxes?
Who really built the Pyramids?
and what's the Sphinx pointing at?
What caused the Big Thaw 12,000 years ago?
Who built Gobekli Tepe?
Can nutrition do more than drugs?
Was there a planet in the Asteroid Belt?
Is there another planet lurking out there?
When will the next comet hit the Earth?
Does the Sun affect the weather
and cause earthquakes?
Why are there so many coincidences about the Moon?
What's under Antarctica?
Is time travel possible?
Have aliens visited our planet?

Why are there so many wars; and
people who support them?
Why do we allow starvation
and homelessness in a world of plenty?
Why is there greed and materialism?
Why does our society put profit before people?
Why don't more people ask
The BIG Questions?

words and music copyright 2016 Anthony Caravan (BMI)
available on iTunes, YouTube, Spotify and most other online music sources

DESPAIR

by Tony Caravan

There's an overwhelming feeling inside
An itching anxiety you can't hide
The stress of life and cost of living
It eats at your body and entire being

You try diversions, media and gaming
But it's always there as an underpinning
Others downplay it and rationalize it
But you know they're just concealing it

DESPAIR—the plague of our culture
Where the greedy and powerful are vultures
Feeding on everything we do
Enslaving us so they can pursue

A life without DESPAIR
Only for the chosen few
The vampires and succubus
Who prosper on us

You try to fight it, you self-medicate
You try to beat it, pray and meditate
You get help and prescriptions drugs
But the next day you're victimized by thugs

There's no escape from the terror
The propagandists say you're in error
They weave and spin and promise better
But in the end you're left in squalor

DESPAIR—has destroyed our culture
The greedy and powerful are vultures
They feed on the fruits of our labors
And keep taking more without a care

continued

Our lives are filled with DESPAIR
When all we want is to be happy
DESPAIR—won't someone set us free?
No more DESPAIR for you and me

words and music copyright 2016 Anthony Caravan (BMI)
available on iTunes, YouTube, Spotify and most other online music sources

SELF-DRIVING CARS

by Tony Caravan

I see self-driving cars are coming out
I guess so people can text and drive
or update their status
What a waste of time...

It's funny how they don't see
that the natural evolution will be
back to mass transportation
So why squander the time in-between?

People have lost their humanity
There's no empathy
The goal should be less work,
less driving and more living

You won't find me in a
self-driving car
In fact, I'm gonna stay off the road
Don't want to risk it all
on a sensor
no, no, no, no

Technology brought us a lot
But it's taken away much more
Now people have forgotten
what it's like to live
live their lives
Live, live their lives

There's no going back
I guess we're headin' for the singularity
The merging of man and machine
Whoopee!

The ancients used technology
The natural kind that is
Understanding how the planet works
without needing a machine

I'm no Luddite, against progress
I'm just sayin' if ain't making
us better people, then
it should be a low priority.

First I'd like to see an end to war
then a focus on feeding the poor
We need to heal the sick
and eliminate the stress of debt

Most problems in this world
are because of money and materialism
People have forgotten how to
enjoy life and be truly happy

Yeah, let them make their self-driving cars
Just keep 'em away from me
I just wanna hang in my yard
with the garden, the sun and the stars

words and music copyright 2016 Anthony Caravan (BMI)
available on iTunes, YouTube, Spotify and most other online music sources

DON'T PANIC!

by Tony Caravan

You lost your job
They're pushing you down
You can't pay the bills
They're taking your stuff
You're hungry and tired
They're makin' you sick

Don't Panic!

They flaunt it on TV
They drive in their SUVs
They live in their mansions
They smirk at you
And call you a bum
They make fun of you

Don't Panic!

There's a fine line they're crossin'
A fringe they're beyond

continued

The castle is crumbling
Dystopia is comin'

Don't Panic!

Humanity has peaked
The next extinction is man
A.I. won't save anyone
Technology is diversion

Don't Panic!

A frog-prince will be king
The queen of hearts will fall
Jack will betray his master
The egg man has fallen

Don't Panic!

Let go of your fears
Open your mind
The answers are around you
You just have to take charge

Don't Panic!

There's a fine line they've crossed
A fringe they're beyond
The castle has crumbled
Dystopia is here

words and music copyright 2016 Anthony Caravan (BMI)
available on iTunes, YouTube, Spotify and most other online music sources

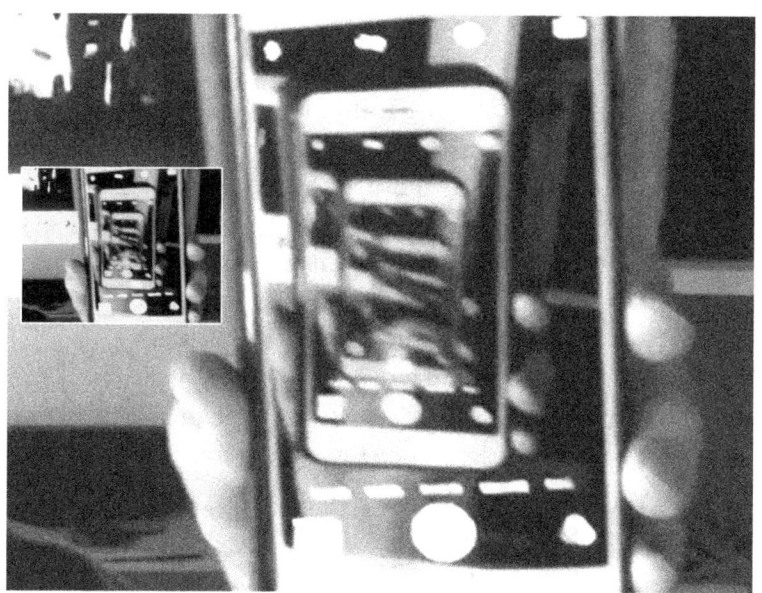

GAME OVER

by Tony Caravan

It's not hard to see that things
have gone from bad to worse—everywhere!
Humanity is clearly on a path
of self-destruction and hopelessness.

Not that things haven't seemed
dreadful before:
Ancient barbarism and slavery,
The Plague, The Holocaust,
and all the wars…

But amid the horror and despair,
in days gone by, there were always
places and people in other parts
of the world that were unaffected.
Places for the fortunate to escape to,
People who were welcoming and who cared.

Now we live in a world of desperation;
where billions of people are suffering,
poor, sick, enslaved and downright unhappy.

continued

Those few who are merry and live well,
do so by taking from the rest of us.
And those who are accepting and content
are as guilty as those who are in charge.

There's no happy ending this time
Because there's no place to run to.
No new country, no land of opportunity.
Each year it gets worse for more and
more people, and only those who are in
pain, seem to see through the lies.

It's as if life is video game and we're
just characters in a virtual world.
We have little control over our limited lives,
while the players are having all the fun.

In fact, some believe that the Universe
is a simulation, and that's the way it is.
And perhaps they're right. And now that
we are starting to realize that it's
all a game, the game is about to end.

In fact it's because we are starting to
realize that it is a game, that it's
all about to end.

GAME OVER.

words and music copyright 2016 Anthony Caravan (BMI)
available on iTunes, YouTube, Spotify and most other online music sources

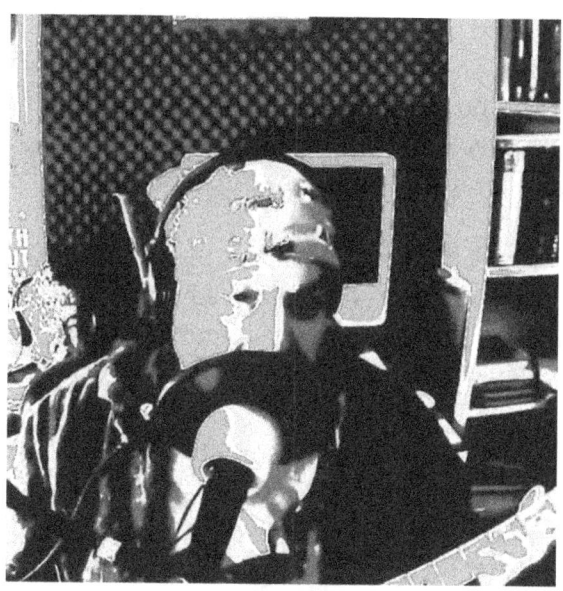

PORTRAIT

by Tony Caravan

The cruelty of this society has no bounds
The lack of empathy by the media and politicians
defies all logic, common sense and decency.
Our humanity has been traded for greed and materialism
Our people are sick and dying and despairing.

The armchair warriors cheer on the chicken-hawks
While young soldiers die in wars
that should never have been fought.
Freedom is being lost at home, not on the battlefields
Our people are dying and injured, afraid and alone.

We're stressed over debts that should never have been
The prices of everything have risen beyond our means
There's no compassion for the struggling millions
Half the nation is stressed and sick, broke without hope.

For every well-dressed person, there are dozens in rags
For everyone living in a mansion, there are thousands in shacks
For everyone going out to eat, there are hundreds starving
For everyone with money in the bank, there are hundreds without.

The media and politicians paint a different picture
They ignore the fact that this is a representative government
They forget that the people actually own this country
They ignore the will of the citizens who pay taxes.

The elections are spectacles of great diversion
The media makes billions on advertising revenue
The politicians are all puppets of their campaign contributors
Most laws of the land are now written by lobbyists.

How we got to this point is simple
The people were diverted by entertainment and wars
We ate and drank and drove and worshipped the pop icons
While the Wall Street criminals secretly took over

There's no going back; they've changed most of the laws
The bureaucracy has grown so big—it's out of control
One thing's for certain, there's no concern for the citizenry
The owners can do just fine printing all the money they need.

That brings us to a pickle,
what to do with the tens of millions
who want to work, but can't find a job?
Or those who worked their whole lives,
but can't afford the bills?
I don't think they think about us,
or even are aware of our suffering
They're too busy living the good life
on our taxes, fees and interest.

words and music copyright 2016 Anthony Caravan (BMI)
available on iTunes, YouTube, Spotify and most other online music sources

I WOKE FROM THE DREAM

by Tony Caravan

Sensory overload
Things have changed so very much
I don't know where to begin,
but I know how it ends

Politicians and money-makers
make their rules for their games
People follow like toy soldiers
and their lives become nothing
but a script from a page

I woke from the dream
and discovered that I
could do whatever I wanted to
And that despite the commands
of the manipulators
I was free, truly free
Free to love, to forgive, to care
to be me

It's hard to focus on the big picture
when there are so many diversions
But reality is all around you
if you step off the merry-go-round

Sensory overflow
Things have changed so very much
I don't know where to begin,
but I know it ends
I know how it ends

Politicians and money-makers
make their rules for their silly games
People follow like toy soldiers
and their lives become nothing
Nothing but a script from a page

words and music copyright 2016 Anthony Caravan (BMI)
available on iTunes, YouTube, Spotify and most other online music sources

Surrealistic Nightmare

PLANET X

by Tony Caravan

Some ten or 12,000 years ago the planet Phaeton
was destroyed by an object entering our solar system
Some say it was a comet, whose water was responsible
for the Great Deluge or Noah's Flood
Others believe Planet Niburu from our Sun's binary star, Nemesis
passes too close every 3,600 years or so
wreaking havoc on the planet's rotation
and magnetic fields

Some say that time has come again, and that's
why we have earthquakes, volcanoes, sink holes,
wild weather and crazy solar activity

In the last great deluge all of the great cities
along the ancient shorelines were covered over by
the ocean—caused by the fast ice melt
This time we don't know what will happen:
Atmospheric and magnetic disruptions or pole shift;
Meteors in the oceans and tsunamis;
The Earth's crust moving, new Arctic and Tropical regions

It comes at a time of great social unrest
Where the majority of the people on the planet
are poor and suffering
Where a few governments and their power-hungry,
greedy leaders prosper on the enslavement of the masses.

For many it's hard to imagine things continuing
this way for too much longer.
The faithful say it's the End Times,
and everyone else is hoping for a miracle

We paid no attention to history,
perhaps the answers were set in stone with the Sphinx
and the Pyramids, and all the other ancient monuments.

continued

The arrogant leaders of the day,
are blinded by their egos,
so we'll never know the truth;
and who knows what they destroyed,
or have displayed
in their private museums and mansions

One thing for certain, something's coming
Something happening now,
and it's gonna get worse soon
If it's Planet X or a comet,
or something completely different.
We're gonna find out soon,
and those who plan to wait it out in their tunnels,
those who don't get flooded underground,
might wake up to a surprising new world
or no world at all

The winds of change are coming and there's
no stopping them

words and music copyright 2016 Anthony Caravan (BMI)
available on iTunes, YouTube, Spotify and most other online music sources

IN ANOTHER TIME AND PLACE

by Tony Caravan

We're all writing songs
We're all writing books
We're all posting this
and we're all tweeting that

We're talking about one thing
and wondering about another
Though it's all been said before
we're not so sure

In another time and place
Somewhere in another time and place

We haven't scratched the surface
of the knowledge that already exists
We're too clouded with the here and now
to be aware of what we don't know

The more we obsess on trivial things
the further behind we get
and harder it will become to learn
We're losing information on daily basis

In another time and place
Somewhere in another time and place

Some argue that knowing things
is not for everyone
And that an education is only good
for those who can use it

I reckon that's true
for plants and cats and kangaroos
But we've grown these brains
capable of so much thinking
it seems like such a waste
to not live to our full potential

In another time and place
Somewhere in another time and place

But I guess there's those
that rather just romp
To play and be entertained
without a care about how things work

Others are cursed with the
burning need to know why
An insatiable quest to comprehend
it all before they die

Perhaps we need to do both
Live, laugh, love and learn
To find a balance to become
wholly human

But one thing's for certain
in this age of information
we're losing the race
and getting very far behind

In another time and place
humans may have evolved
to comprehend it all
while being compassionate
and one with the natural world

But it's clear we're on a
dead-end path
of self-centeredness
where only a few will
truly experience what it
means to be a part of
this Universe.

Maybe, in another time and place
Somewhere in another time and place

A SHARP SWORD

by Tony Caravan

You are not free.
You are merely presented with
choices that all have predetermined outcomes.

We don't see the stars.
We miss the sunrises and sunsets.
We have little appreciate for fine art.
We ignore the human condition
and the quality of life
(for most people on the planet)
has become subpar at best.

We have become self-centered drones
controlled by cell phone towers and WiFi hotspots
that broadcast commands
by corporations, banksters and politicians.

The human animal adapts to more and more work
and less and less humanity.

We have become slaves—prisoners in gilded cages.

You are not free. You are merely presented with
choices that all have predetermined outcomes.

Affection and thought, love and wisdom…

A sharp sword coming out of the mouth of the sun

You are not free. You are merely presented with
choices that all have predetermined outcomes.

words and music copyright 2016 Anthony Caravan (BMI)
available on iTunes, YouTube, Spotify and most other online music sources

FORGOTTEN PEOPLE

by Tony Caravan

All around the world
there are people sitting alone,
broken and struggling,
because society kept them down.

Maybe they didn't come from money,
or maybe their look's just not right,
Could be a victim of circumstances,
or just out of the public sight.

But I'm not talking just about
the downtrodden and the poor,
—they've got it real bad too.
I'm talking about the talented
and forgotten people that
could have made life better
for me and you.

We elevated the wrong people
to the top of the food chain;
and left behind the ones
who know better
and have the ability to make real change.

It's a backwards culture,
where the rich and powerful rule;
and those with the greatest minds
are simply left behind.

It's a sad, sad story,
that's been told a thousand times;
just not so much recently,
and that's the real crime.

continued

For at least if we know
about the tragic heroes of our age,
then dreams hold hope,
and tears can be soothed.

Instead we're lost
in a techno-obsessed world,
where greed and deceit
are the most rewarded.

Cry for the lost souls
the forgotten ones
and maybe, just maybe,
a few will be found.

There's no future
in a world without them,
just empty diversions
and holograms.

Yeah, I'm not talking just about
the downtrodden and the poor,
they've got it real bad too;
I'm talking about the talented
and forgotten people that
could have made life better
for me and you.

words and music copyright 2016 Anthony Caravan (BMI)
available on iTunes, YouTube, Spotify and most other online music sources

HOLIDAYS IN DYSTOPIA

by Tony Caravan

I trampled a little over a mile in the cold;
back from the nearby grocery store,
past the abandoned buildings, (and)
over the snow and ice-covered sidewalks.
Carrying my plastic bag of manager's specials:
stale bread, ends meat, processed cheese,
a box of scary cat food, a carrot and a potato.
This would have to sustain the two of us
for the entire holiday weekend.

The power has long since been turned off.
Good thing I installed the wood stove,
and bought that solar panel to charge my power pack.
There should be just enough juice
to listen to some music by the fire
while he have our holiday dinner.

Haven't had the internet or a phone or TV
in over a year, so I don't hear much
from people, or know what's going on.

I hear the cars go by—the lucky ones
those who found, or still have jobs.

I guess I'll just hope they don't kick
me out of the house,
there are so many people now who have defaulted on their loans,
I figure it might take months or years
for them to get around to every foreclosure.

Time to bundle up by the fire
and get ready to try and sleep.

Another holiday—cold and alone.

What year is it? 2016? 2017? I can't recall.

Surrealistic Nightmare

TWEETS & QUOTES

@realTonyCaravan

Surrealistic Nightmare

All the politicians do is keep asking you for more donations... it's crazy! Everyday my email is full of them. Anyway... if you really want to support something, support the arts and the people pointing out the truth.

....

I've decided to stop using credit cards. I have (had) nine of them. The temptation for buying unnecessary things is just too strong with plastic; and it's wasteful. Besides, where do they get off charging the interest rates they do, when they get their money for free?!

....

There is a distinct possibility, backed up by the observable weather extremes, that **we're not so much dealing with Climate "Change" as much as a Climate Crisis.** In the latter instance, there are no rules... the jet stream behaves erratically, more variations in temperatures, floods and droughts, storms, etc... Watch the Sun...

....

Mankind has further fulfilled its purpose by injecting even more carbon dioxide and methane into the atmosphere. **We're basically made to exhale and excrete waste.** Our ultimate purpose on Earth.

....

The backlash of the politico-corporate-bankster take over will be the expansion of nihilism. More and more people will be moving toward the existential idea of living in their own world. This will be the clash of civilizations that the powers that be never calculated into their 21st Century theocratic-feudalism plan.

....

I'm already there... **I don't believe in any of them anymore—or their silly suits and societal structures.** They are not real; ergo: they can no longer control or affect me. I will not be brought down by the insane people who believe they own and rule this world— not in my world.

....

People choose personalities like clothing; but underneath they're something different. Likewise people are attracted to an image not the essence.

....

The side effect of advertising, public relations, the education system and political campaigns is the inability of many people to discern the truth from an assertion, or claim. This is compounded by repeated exposure, by the media, of the pop cultural icons of the day—which has created the modern day "cult of personality."

Furthermore, as people begin to worship their, so called, leaders; they end up believing practically everything they say. And finally, they mold their own personalities to mimic those whom they look up to. **Ultimately, they become carbon copies of a persona that was manufactured for the sole purpose of manipulating the public.**

More and more people are becoming unwitting victims of the culture industry, and when confronted with this reality, their response can only be described as one of **cognitive dissonance**.

The only way to reverse this process, unfortunately, would be to use the same methodology and media to get the truth about reality out to the masses. The problem with that, is that **it's just another form of messing with people's heads.**

My advice is to adhere to the old Edgar Allan Poe quote, **"Believe only half of what you see and nothing that you hear."**

Best advice for someone struggling with a decision:
"The only person standing in your way is YOU." —Black Swan

#Twitter should have a clickable "bull" below tweets for the obvious reason.

Most under-reported #news story this year is the financial struggle & stress of majority of U.S. pop. **Reporters living too comfy to feel it.**

Amazing how **#banks can literally create money out of thin air,** loan it, charge interest, and if your late, sell your property for profit.

Media have become "tabloid journalists." Instead of dealing w/ real issues of high rents, debt, our struggle, they provoke & sensationalize.

Even those we vehemently disagree with got to that place for a reason. **Problem solving only works when we delve into other points of view.**

Problems are beyond left-right, B&W, rich-poor. It's media-driven focus on one issue at a time that prevents us from seeing the big picture.

Surrealistic Nightmare

A reduction in rents, utilities & other fixed expenses is necessary to maintain the consumer #economy—besides being the humane thing to do.

....

One of the coolest things about owning your own house is that you can play #loud #music early in the morning or late at night.

....

"I took off my watch and found I had all the time in the world..."
—Time for Livin' by The Association

....

The idea that insurance companies, utilities, telecoms, et al. can keep raising prices—unchecked—is not only insanity, it's feudalism.

....

Don't you just love it when you get paid & realize that even if you don't pay your bills in full, you still have nothing left. #wage-slavery

....

Considering #lobbyist influence, potential for #veto overrides, DC bureaucratic culture, et al., **the #campaign cycle distracts the country for two years.**

....

Corporatists decry pay-to-play social programs, but they are the first to accept free #corporate welfare, #bailouts & gov't protections. Hmm...

....

It's mind-boggling how the media ignores that over a hundred million people in this country #struggle to pay their rent, bills, fees & meds.

....

All you really need to do to #survive is to eat and drink. It's funny (and sad) how many other "needful things" our society has tacked on.

....

Most of the answers to the "big questions" are available; however they are either not being asked, or not available via #search or #media.

....

Candidates promise to create "order out of chaos." This is an ancient deception. The media blinds us with lies as each year things get worse

....

more

Not doing the right thing because of job losses is absurd. Displaced workers should be compensated if it means saving lives and the planet.

Most don't know that banks and corps are buying up #properties (and inflating prices). The goal? A move toward a #renter/leasee society.

My bank is now charging customers 1.5%+ interest for the privilege of having a checking account. That's a negative interest rate. insane!

The whole idea of working the best hours of the day, for the entire week, and still being broke is nothing short of #slavery. No humanity!

If the banks can get 0 interest rates, why can't we? If gov't can bail out banks, corps and buy their stocks, why can't we get bailed out?

We have to resign ourselves (to) that the majority of people are swayed by the media & cult of personality. Meaning money/fame wins (again).

#Peace is easy, peace is free... We've got to get the profit out of #war and use those trillions of dollars nicely.

The conquest began by putting a #smartphone with GPS & Facebook in everyone's hands. **The takeover is occurring now.**

To the 100+ million U.S. taxpayers who's #wages or salaries don't cover the cost of living and require indebtedness; you are a #slave.

The first step to fixing a broken system is acknowledging it's broken. Next ignore deniers. Then affect positive change beginning with YOU.

In the process of cancelling all credit cards, swapping cell service for #VoIP $35/yr. Growing veggies, scaling down TV ch... enjoying life.

What government #stats, politicians & media don't emphasize is that every 10% is over 32 million people. **Fractions = human beings suffering.**

Another way of looking at household #income figures released today: **43.1 million in #poverty; 29 million without #medical coverage, etc...**

....

work-eat-sleep, work-eat-sleep, work-eat-sleep, work-eat-sleep, work-eat-sleep, work-eat-sleep-play, work-eat-sleep-pay, work-eat-sleep...

....

Success is Failure.

....

"I don't want to survive, I want to live." A great line from the the movie 12 YEARS A SLAVE. Something that the politicians just don't get.

....

It's **hygge** that I miss the most in this post-social media culture that has taken over...

....

It's hard for most people to wrap their head around the idea that current U.S. #propaganda, in many ways, is worse than in Cold War USSR.

....

People believe what they want to believe, and the media and politicians play on this. Most people are afraid of the truth -- it's too scary.

....

There's the media-hyped-stock-buy-back oligarch #economy; and there's the people's economy of debt & #inflation. They don't need us anymore.

....

Daily #debt stress for (most) people is growing & expanding; while media & politicians pretend life is peachy in U.S. (like it is for them).

....

The idea that people get caught up in the #news, the same way they do an episodic TV show, is absurd. Live YOUR life. Experience & feel.

....

We take ocean #sand for granted. It's used for buildings, roads, computers, plastics... And dredging kills fish & habitats & erodes beaches.

....

more

Monthly payments (for practically everything) are absurd. It demonstrates how we really are just cattle on a tax farm that has strict rules.

My relatively new #Mac with 16 gigs of DRAM starts up like an old #Windows machine—and it's streamlined. #Bloatware is very frustrating.

You're free to choose your own scene; and, if you play a game, to play by your rules. We give media & politicians too much power over us.

You'll never see the big picture if you succumb to media & politicians diverting you by focusing on one issue at a time. It's more complex!

The U.S. infrastructure—especially outside of major cities—is simply not safe for a #DriverlessCar; and won't be for decades. Stop!

If politicians and people in the media had #empathy, the world would change for the better; of course, there'd be no more #war profiteering.

Many have said it before, in many ways; but it bears repeating: **humans suffer from mass insanity.** Need proof? Watch, listen or read the news

There is a move to remove the ban on the sale of ivory. Elephants are intelligent creatures. Will man's inhumanity ever end? War, killing...

The idea that humans are the pinnacle of life's achievement on Earth (& the Universe) is both arrogant & absurd. Our species is a failure.

The problem with promises by #politicians & #social movements is that (unfortunately) more than **1/2 the people are mentally gone.** Game over!

#Politicians ask for money to get elected (it goes to media & hotels); then they take more of our money in #taxes (it goes to corps & wars).

The complications of ordinary life due to funny #money & #interest rates on #loans that #banks pull out of thin air, is ridiculous & cruel.

Stop already with 1% v 99%—it's the 80-20 rule that applies. 20% are living comfortable; and it only takes a little more to elect.

Poverty & ignorance of billions of people is thwarting future technologies and destroying the very fabric of modern societies and economies.

Money is paper; politicians are slogans; work is wage-slavery; the media sold out; laws benefit big businesses; our lives have become absurd

Funny thing about #AI, robotics, computer algorithms... **they're all imitations of life** - false realities. I prefer human interaction.

You can't have sanity, peace & calm at gunpoint & with unjust laws. It's time to address the real issues - people are struggling to survive.

I've come to accept that people are either in denial, too dumbed-down, or just so high they can't see (or care) how we're being screwed over

The whole idea that life revolves around paying bills is absurd. The fact that nothing is being done about the stress it causes is criminal.

Millions die of curable or preventable diseases, while bio-genetic breakthroughs are extending the #lifespans of those who can afford it.

There should be an end to new construction until all of the existing buildings are refurbished and/or empty office spaces & housing filled.

Historically, the pacifists and decent folk were remembered and revered far longer than the greedy, power-hungry warriors.

When will people stop liking & believing politicians & media just because they smile or look happy? That doesn't make the bad they do good.

more

Politicians/Civil Servants would be exemplary; if so many weren't puppets of special interest money/campaign contributions, i.e., graft.

"For we wrestle... against powers, against rulers of the darkness of this world, against... wickedness in high places." a 3,000+ yr. old quote

"What if we choose to exist purely in a reality of our own making? Does that render us insane? ...isn't that better than a life of despair?"

Our reliance on machines, robots & algorithms is increasing exponentially. Even the service workers will be replaced. No jobs in the future.

Ancients took a census to charge #taxes; royals stole; colonists #enslaved; **now we have monthly bills. How'd we let them get away with that?**

The news today is absurd; yesterday it was madness, while the day before it was inconceivable (to me). I realize most don't see it that way.

The root of most #inequality & injustice (& lack of true freedom) stems from the cost of living, taxes, services, etc. Stuff costs too much!

Ask hawks why they wage wars & they'll say to protect us. Truth is, **war is about profit from weapons, oil, etc.** Stop that + meddling = peace

It's mind-boggling how billions of people's lives are determined by so few. In the U.S. a few thousand run the lives of over 300 million.

I have no #tweet today.

When politicians say it's complicated, that means they're hiding something. When gov't says nat'l security, it means protecting corporations

U.S. #internet costs are double that of many other advanced nations, yet way slower in speed. Another way Americans get screwed over monthly

---

If the average person knew 1/10th of what #politicians & banksters were up to; well, they wouldn't believe—and they don't. Diversions...

I'm nobody, living in the middle of nowhere, and I've come to the realization that nobody cares what I do or say; only what the media beams.

At the end of the day, #media & #politicians are irrelevant. Ultimately we are the instruments of change on an individual & local level.

Social media is neither media nor social; it's a virtual reality playground taken far too seriously while on the "outside" it gets worse.

"Imagine a country, a world, a time and place, where who the leaders are, and the political news didn't matter... *Guess what?* That time and place is right now.

You can affect positive change in your home, neighborhoods and communities starting today. Forget the politicians, change starts with a groundswell by the people."

@realTonyCaravan

ABOUT THE AUTHOR

Tony Caravan has written a number of books, screenplays, countless articles and songs. He has worked in film, video, radio, publishing, advertising, design, entertainment, education and on the internet.

He is semi-retired, living in a small house, in a small town with a cat, books, computers, musical instruments and a backyard garden and pond.

Inquiries and communications can be made through his website at RockFlux.com

self-portrait with cap, fall 2016

OTHER TITLES BY THE AUTHOR...

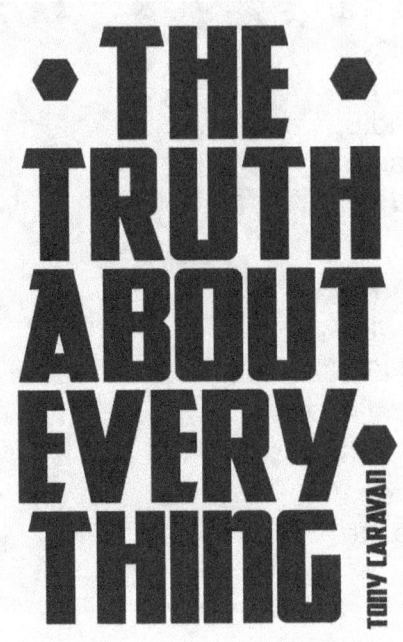

The Truth About Everything

ISBN-13: 978-1519552662

available at bookstores
and online at Amazon.com

also available digitally
on the iTunes bookstore

Handbook for the Upheaval

ISBN-13: 978-1514223772

available at bookstores
and online at Amazon.com

also available digitally
on the iTunes bookstore

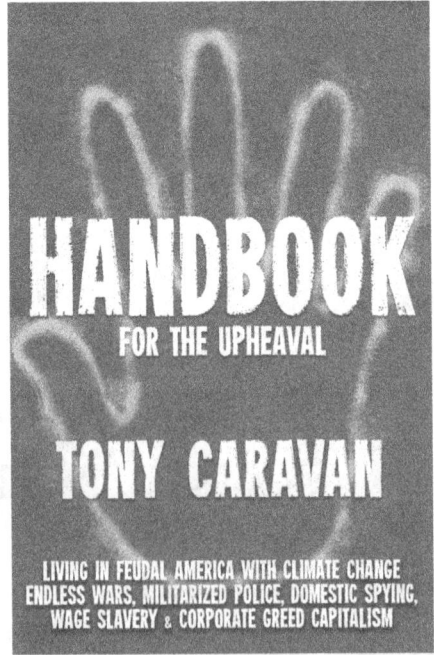

The Non-Conformist

ISBN-13: 978-1500469498

available at bookstores
and online at Amazon.com

also available digitally
on the iTunes bookstore

The Early Years

ISBN-13: 978-1496066428

available at bookstores
and online at Amazon.com

also available digitally
on the iTunes bookstore

ALL MUSIC AVAILABLE ON ITUNES®

Listen on Spotify, YouTube, Amazon Music and your favorite online and on-air stations.

Tony Caravan

Surrealistic Nightmare

The Non-Conformist

ISBN-13: 978-1500469498

available at bookstores
and online at Amazon.com

also available digitally
on the iTunes bookstore

The Early Years

ISBN-13: 978-1496066428

available at bookstores
and online at Amazon.com

also available digitally
on the iTunes bookstore

ALL MUSIC AVAILABLE ON ITUNES®

Listen on Spotify, YouTube, Amazon Music and your favorite online and on-air stations.

www.ingramcontent.com/pod-product-compliance
Lightning Source LLC
Chambersburg PA
CBHW070116290526
45789CB00005B/2037